Chess
for Children

Chess for Children

Sabrina Chevannes

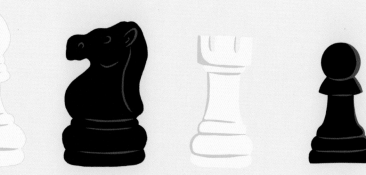

BATSFORD

First published in the United Kingdom in 2013

This reillustrated edition first published in the United Kingdom in 2022 by

B. T. Batsford Ltd
43 Great Ormond Street
London
WC1N 3HZ

An imprint of B. T. Batsford Holdings Limited

ISBN 978 1 84994 729 9

A CIP catalogue record for this book is available from the British Library.

10 9 8 7 6 5 4 3 2 1

Reproduction by Rival Colour, UK
Printed and bound by Toppan Leefung Printing Ltd, China

Illustrations by Naomi Wilkinson

Contents

Introduction

Hi, my name is Jess!

Hi, my name is Jamie!

And we're going to teach you everything we know about chess!

Jamie: Chess is our favourite game in the world, and we want everyone to learn how to play so they can play with us. So, in this book, we'll tell you everything we know about chess and, by the time you finish reading, you will be as good at it as us!

Jess: I love chess because it's a game that lots of really clever people play. So everyone says I'm really clever because I'm good at chess.

Jamie: I love chess because I like fighting games. I know it's not nice to fight with other people, so I fight over the chessboard!

Jess: Chess helps me to calculate and think properly, so it also helps me with my schoolwork! My memory has got much better since playing chess, and I can work out problems in a much better way now, too!

Jamie: I just like to win! Winning makes me feel good. Since chess is a battle of the minds, if I beat someone at chess, it makes me feel like I'm cleverer than them, and that's a good feeling!

Jess: Chess is a battle game between two armies – the white and black armies. They have to fight against each other in order to trap the other army's king and take over their kingdom.

Jamie: Yeah, and the person who does this first gets to shout 'CHECKMATE' and they win the game!

Jess: But we don't shout, though, Jamie, remember? Chess is supposed to be a quiet game.

Jamie: Oh, I keep forgetting that! Shhhhhhhh!

Jess: Chess has been around for hundreds and hundreds of years and still has never been mastered. This is one of the things that makes the game so fantastic!

Jamie: Chess originated in India before 500AD, then the Persians heard about it and started playing it, too. Chess didn't make its way over to Europe until about the 12th century, and then we started playing competitive chess only in the 1800s.

Wow! You know a lot about the history of chess, Jamie!
Well, it is my favourite game! Let's learn more about the battlefield.

The Battlefield

The chess battlefield is known as the chessboard. It's square in shape and split into little light and dark squares:

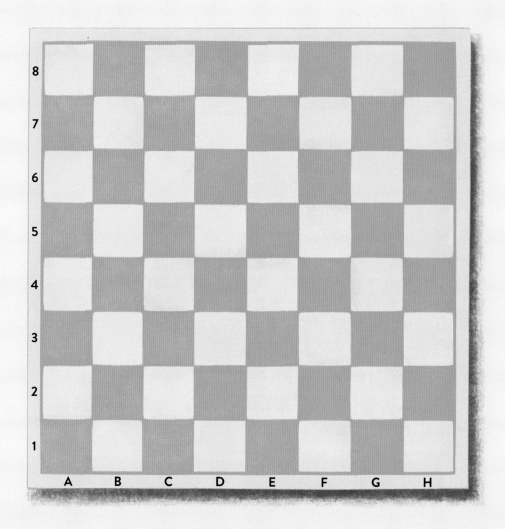

Jamie: The chessboard has 64 little squares, to be precise. I know this because there are eight squares along the bottom and eight squares up the sides. 8 x 8 = 64!

Jess: OK smartypants, that's very clever, but did you know that the lines up and down the chessboard have special names? So do the ones that go across the chessboard.

Jamie: Yeah, they are called rows.

Jess: No they are not. You can *call* them rows, but in chess, we use special names for them. The ones that go up and down the board are called **files** and are named after letters.

Jamie: I've heard that word before. When the teachers tell us to line up outside, they ask us to stand in single file!

Jess: Yes, exactly. You see the one highlighted here? This one is called the e-file, because it is all the squares above the letter e on the chessboard.

Jamie: Ah yes, because we have letters and numbers on the sides of our chessboards to help us name the squares.

Jess: We'll get to that in a minute, Jamie, but do you know what the rows across the chessboard are called?

Jamie: No! I thought they were just called rows.

Jess: No, they are called **ranks** and they are named after numbers.

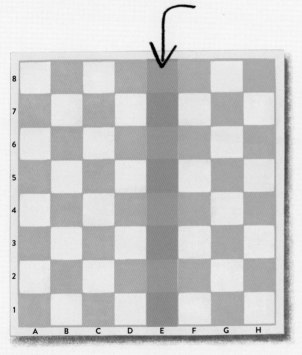

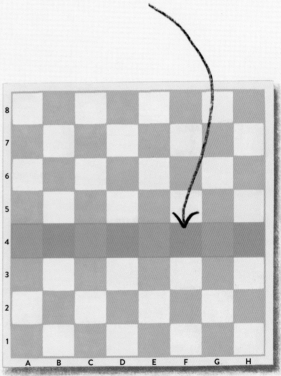

Jamie: So the rank in the diagram is called the 4th rank, because the squares that are highlighted are all on the row with the number 4 by it.

Jess: Exactly – nice and easy! There's another line on the chessboard we often describe. This one goes at an angle and is called a **diagonal**.

Jamie: And we call this diagonal the a1–h8 diagonal because of the squares that it passes through.

Jess: What do you mean a1–h8? Why this?

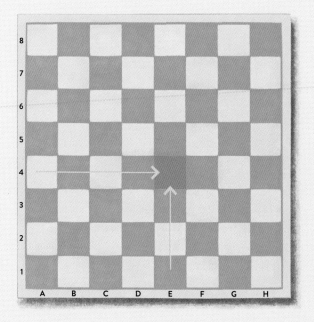

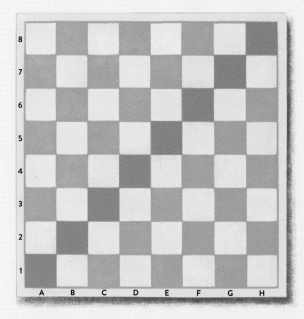

Jamie: They are the names of the squares! Each square has its own name, represented by one letter and one number, which are called the co-ordinates. In this diagram, to work out which square is highlighted, first I'd look at the bottom of the board to see which letter the square is above. Then I'd follow the row to the side of the board to see which number row it is, and would discover that the co-ordinate of the square is e4.

Jess: Ah yes, I remember now! They're like the postcodes of each of the squares. I think of the squares as little homes for the pieces, and that their co-ordinate is their address.

Jamie: Whatever works for you, Jess! Just remember that it's important to be able to understand chess co-ordinates, because this is how all games are recorded and how chess professionals talk to each other. So you must be able to master chess co-ordinates if you want to understand what these people mean!

Jess: All of this terminology – rank, file, diagonal, the co-ordinates, is **chess language**. We'll use these terms throughout the book.

Jamie: What about how we set up the board? I want to know how to do that before we start.

Jess: Well, we'll come to that later. We don't know what all the pieces are yet!

Jamie: OK, but I'm going to include a diagram of what the starting position looks like, just in case we need it.

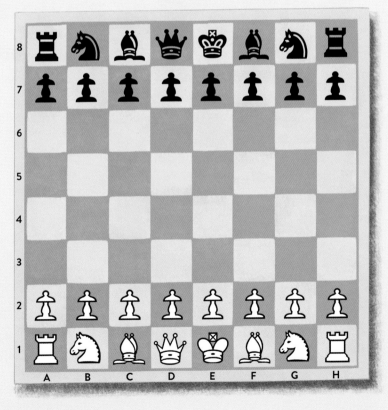

The Pawn

Jamie: The pawn is the smallest soldier in our chess army. He doesn't get to move very far, and can only go forward. He usually only moves one square at a time, but on his very first move, he can choose to move two squares if he wants to. Once he has moved, he can definitely only go one square at a time after that. Look:

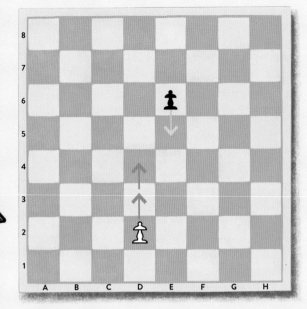

You see that the white pawn hasn't moved yet, because he's on his starting position. Well, he can choose to move either one square or two squares – to either d3 or d4. But the black pawn has already moved, so he doesn't have a choice and can only move forward by one square.

Jess: Why is the black pawn going backward? I thought you said they can only go forward?!

Jamie: It IS going forward! Remember, the two armies play toward each other, so the black army will be going forward toward the 1st rank, and the white army will be going forward toward the 8th rank.

Jess: Oh, OK, I get it now! However, I think you've forgotten something, Jamie...

Jamie: No I haven't! That's *everything* about how the pawns move.

Jess: No it's not – I know something else:

Even though the pawns are very small, they are quite complicated because they move differently from the way they capture. If they want to capture another piece, they have to do so **diagonally**, and only one square diagonally.

Jamie: What are you talking about, Jess?!

Jess: Look:

Imagine this situation – the white pawn is right next to three black pawns that are all right in front of it. Which one can it take?

Jamie: The one on d5, of course – because it can only move forward.

Jess: Wrong! The pawn captures differently from the way it moves, remember! The pawn can capture any opposing pawn that is diagonally one square away from him. So he can choose to take either the pawn on c5 or e5, but **not** the one on d5!

Jamie: Wow, pawns *are* complicated! Thanks Jess. Now I really do know everything about how the pawn moves.

Jess: Not quite, Jamie. There's more, but I'll talk about that later in the book. For now, I'll just remind you that we attach a points value to the pieces – and pawns are considered to be worth the least out of all of the army, since they are the smallest.

Jamie: How many points are the pawns worth then, Jess?

Jess: Only one point. They can only go forward, never backward, and they can only move a limited number of squares.

Jamie: Wow, that's harsh! But we have eight pawns at the beginning of the game. Now that's a lot of pawns!

Jess: Exactly! There's strength in numbers. So the whole army of pawns is worth eight points, but alone they are only worth one.

Pawns, not Prawns!

Remember – these little soldiers are great warriors that will be loyal to your army and protect their fellow men whenever they can. They are NOT little crustaceans that spice up your soup or salad. I do NOT want to see you eating the pawns!

Pawn Wars

Jamie: There's a really cool game that I like to play with the pawns called **Pawn Wars**.

Jess: That sounds cool! How do you play?

Jamie: First of all, you set up all the pawns on the correct squares, where they start at the beginning of the game. The white pawns must all line up on the **2nd rank** and the black pawns must all line up on the **7th rank**.

The rules of the game are then quite easy. White goes first, since White always moves first in a game of chess. You can win in three different ways:

1. Get a pawn to the end of the board before your opponent.

2. Capture all of your opponent's pawns.

3. Make your opponent run out of moves.

The third way is the hardest because if you try to stop your opponent from moving, you may block your own pawns, so be careful!

Jess: That sounds like a great way to practise our pawn moves. Let's have a game now!

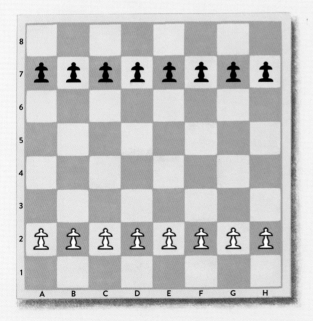

The Rook

Jamie: I want to learn about a faster piece now. The pawns were too slow for me. Luckily we have eight of them to play with!

Jess: Well, the rook is a much faster piece than the pawn. He can move as many squares as he likes, as long as nothing is in his way.

Jamie: Wow, that sounds much better! Can he move in any direction he likes?

Jess: No, he must move in straight lines only. He can go forward, backward and sideways – not diagonally.

Jamie: He makes a sort of a 'plus' sign with his moves, like in maths.

Jess: Yes, but he can't change direction when he moves – he must choose which direction he is to go in. He can go forward or backward or left or right, not a mixture.

Jamie: Does he capture differently from the way he moves, like the pawns do?

Jess: No, it's only the pawns that do that. The rest of the pieces capture the same way as they move.

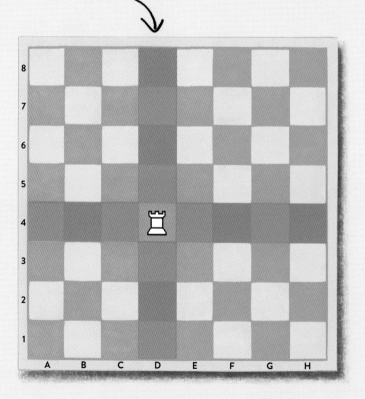

Jamie: Phew! That makes it a lot easier to learn then.

Jess: Yes, if the rook lands on a piece of the opposing team, then it can capture it, but it can't keep moving past that piece.

So, in this position, if the rook was to capture the pawn, it would land on g4, but couldn't then move to h4 in the same go. He would have to stay on g4, but does get to remove the black pawn from the board.

Jamie: I like the rook. Did you know that, in many countries, the rook represents a chariot? Even in Chinese chess, there's a piece that moves in a similar way to a rook, and it's called a chariot!

Jess: Yes, but I think in most European countries, the rook represents a tower, which is why our piece looks the way it does.

Jamie: And why some people call it a castle!

Jess: Exactly! We must remember not to call it a castle, though, and use its real name – rook. Even though it does look a bit like a castle!

Rampant Rooks

Jess: Do you know any games we can play to practise moving the rooks, just as we practised the pawn movements by playing Pawn Wars?

Jamie: Yes, I like to play **Pawn Hunt** with the rooks. The game is simple. We each get one rook and we place them in opposite corners of the board – rooks both sit in the corners at the beginning of the game. Then we put all of our own pawns on the board, wherever we like. The object of the game is to capture all of our opponent's pawns before they capture ours! The pawns can't move, so we can focus on just moving our rooks correctly.

An example starting position for the Pawn Hunt:

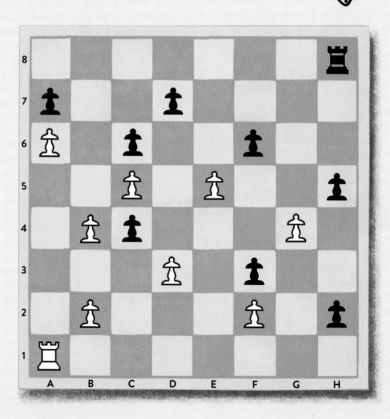

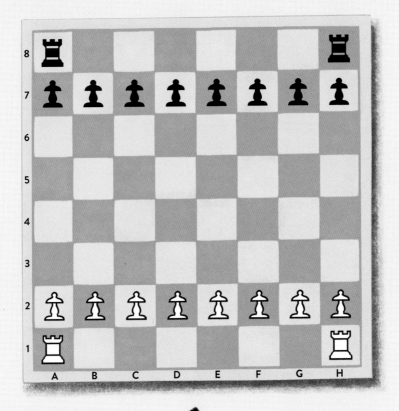

Jess: Can the rooks get each other?

Jamie: Yes! So be careful not to put your rook in the way of your opponent's. Remember that if you are attacking them, they are also attacking you!

Jess: It sounds really fun! Is there anything else we can play?

Jamie: Well, I also like to play a mini-game with just the rooks and pawns all in their starting positions.

Jess: Oh, I've played that before! We get to play with both rooks and all eight pawns, and they all start where they are supposed to at the beginning of a game. Then the first person to capture all of the opponent's pieces wins.

Jamie: Yes, that's correct. There's also another way of winning. If we get a pawn safely to the end of the board, then we also win.

Jess: What do you mean by safely?

Jamie: Well, I mean so that the opponent can't capture it immediately. The opponent gets one more go to see if he can capture the pawn. If he can, in just one move, the game continues. If not, then you win!

Jess: Fantastic! Let's play some of these games now!

The Bishop

Jess: The bishop is the piece that looks a bit like a big pawn, except it has a groove in its head. This groove is supposed to represent the mitre (the bishop's hat).

Jamie: Yeah, the bishop is a bit of a strange one, because different countries had different names for it as they thought it represented different things. In Romania and France, their name for it means 'fool'.

Jess: Yes, they thought the bishop looked more like a jester, and that the groove was the jester's cap!

Jamie: I don't think it looks anything like a jester! They are too silly to be bishops!

Jess: Well, the bishop can only move diagonally, so it's much more limited than the rook, but still a lot faster than the pawn.

Jamie: Can it also go backward though?

Jess: Yes, all of the chess pieces can go backward, apart from the pawn.

Jamie: Grrr, that pawn! At least we have eight of them...

Jess: But we only have two bishops! One of them starts on a white square and the other starts on a black square. So they can never meet or land on the same square.

Jamie: Why not?

Jess: Because if they only move diagonally, they have to stick to the colour of the square on which they started, so they can't move onto the opposite colour squares.

Jamie: Oh yeah!! That's good to remember! The word diagonally reminds me of that place in Harry Potter... What was it called?

Jess: Diagon Alley! The place that was invisible to Muggles, the non-magical people. That's a great way of remembering how the bishop moves, Jamie.

Jamie: I love Harry Potter!

Jess: Well, we can also remember how it moves as a multiplication sign, like in maths.

Jamie: Just how the rook made the 'plus' sign!

Jess: Yes, exactly!

Jamie: The bishop seems a bit rubbish, though, if it can only go on one colour square. Although, I suppose, it's faster than a pawn.

Jess: Well, those are its strengths and weaknesses right there. It can travel quite fast and move backward, but anything on the opposite colour square is safe from the bishop.

Busy Bishops

Jamie: To practise the bishop moves, we can play the same sort of games we played for the rooks. We can play **Pawn Hunt** with the bishops!

Jess: Great idea! We should set up the bishops on the squares they start on at the beginning of the game, and place all eight of our pawns wherever we want.

Jamie: I've got to remember that the white bishops always start on c1 and f1, and the black bishops on c8 and f8.

Jess: And you have to remember that the pawns don't move in Pawn Hunt. And that White always goes first!

Jamie: We can also play a mini-game with our bishops and pawns as we did with the rooks on page 21!

Jess: Yes, let's play that now and let's set up the board like this:

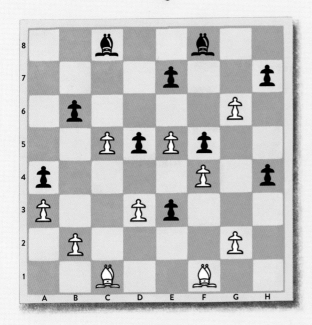

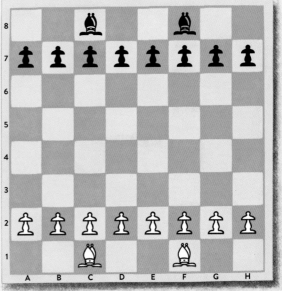

The Queen

Jess: Yay! We are going to talk about my favourite piece now! The queen!

Jamie: Why is she your favourite piece, Jess?

Jess: Because she's like a bishop and a rook put together. She's super-fast!

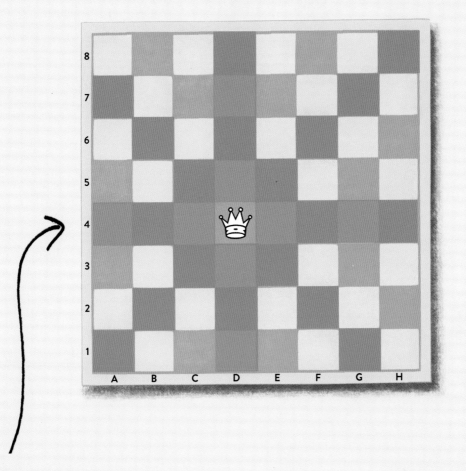

Jamie: She's pretty cool – she can move forward, backward, sideways, diagonally... Have I forgotten anything?

Jess: Nope, that sounds like her! She's so cool. She's the most powerful piece in our army, because she can move as many squares as she likes in so many directions!

Jamie: Wow! I've just counted. When she sits in the middle of the board and nothing is in her way, she controls 27 different squares! That's almost half of the squares on the chessboard.

Jess: Yup! She's amazing!

Quirky Queens

Jamie: I have the coolest game to practise the queen moves. It's more difficult than the other ones because it needs a lot more calculation. The game is called **Cops and Robbers**.

Jess: Ooh, interesting! How do you play?

Jamie: Well, you begin the game with one queen on its starting square. The queen is the cop and all the opponent's pawns are the robbers. You must capture all of the robbers before they make it to the other side of the board safely. If a robber makes it to the other side of the board before you can get him, then you lose the game. However, if you capture all the robbers in time, then you win the game!

Jess: That sounds really fun! Do you get another go to capture the pawn immediately if they make it to the other side of the board?

Jamie: Yes, the robbers need to make it to the other side *safely*.

Jess: One thing – you mention that the queen must begin the game on her starting square. How do you know which square this is?

Jamie: You know the answer to that, Jess!

Jess: I know, I was just checking to see if you did. Hee hee!

Jamie: I know – the queen always goes on her own colour square.

Jess: And do you know why?

Jamie: Because those are the rules!

Jess: Yes, those are the rules, but it's because the queen is a very fashionable lady. She always dresses amazingly. Her accessories always match. Whenever she goes out, she must match the colour of her dress with her shoes and her handbag, so she must match the colour square she starts on with whatever colour she is.

Jamie: Ah, she's a very stylish lady indeed!

Jess: You will also notice that she starts on the d-file. This is because she loves diamonds.

Jamie: I see, D for diamonds!

Jess: OK, so this board is now set up for Cops and Robbers, so let's get started!

Jamie: Remember, White goes first! So don't go nabbing my d-pawn straight away. I have a chance to defend it first. And if you lose your queen, then the game is over! I only need to get one pawn to the end of the board, so I fancy my chances.

The Knight

Jess: The knight is the most complicated piece on the chessboard. It doesn't move in a straight line or just one direction.

Jamie: No it's not, it's easy. You're just stupid.

Jess: Now Jamie, that's just rude. Name-calling is definitely not allowed in chess.

Jamie: Sorry Jess. I just love knights – they're my favourite piece.

Jess: Doesn't mean they're easy to master, though.

Jamie: That's true; they are very tricky to understand.

Jess: The knight moves in an L-shape so has to change direction, which makes it more difficult to understand. This knight sits on c3 and can go to d5 in one move. It can actually do so in two different ways, shown by the yellow and red arrows. They always go two in one direction and then one in another, but it's very confusing! There are usually two different ways to get to a square, so sometimes you can go one square in one direction and then two in another.

Jamie: I'll tell you the way I remember the knight move to make it easier for myself. The knight is a lot like a horse – the chess piece also looks like a horse, so I think of its movement as a horse's movement. The knight goes 'clippety-clop and around the corner'. So the clippety-clop is the two squares and then it goes around the corner for the last square.

Jess: That's a clever way of remembering it. I'll try it! Though I guess the clippety-clop thing doesn't quite work when we go one square

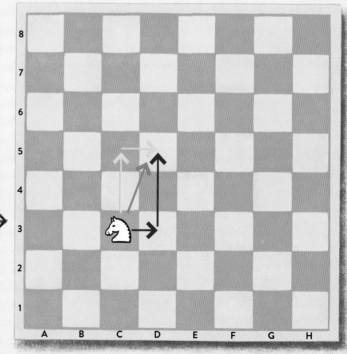

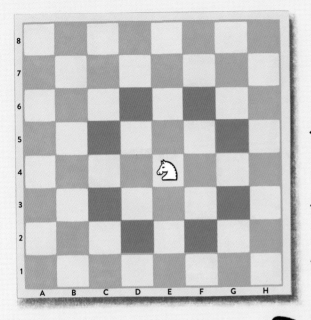

Jess: No, I didn't notice that! Does that mean that if it starts on a black square, it can only go to a white square?

Jamie: Yes, exactly! It's a good thing to remember.

Jess: The knight is so special – nothing can move like a knight. It's a really unique piece.

Jamie: It also has another power that none of the other pieces have – it can jump!

Jess: It really is like a horse!

then two. Maybe we can just clippety-clop backward. I know, I'll put a knight in the middle of the board and see how many squares it controls from that square. I found eight different squares by going 'clippety-clop and around the corner'!

Jamie: That's all of them! And you will notice that it makes a circle around the knight.

Jess: It's an Octopus Knight!

Jamie: Huh?!

Jess: An octopus has eight legs; the knight is controlling eight squares all around itself. It's like an octopus!

Jamie: Ah, I see! An Octopus Knight! Did you also notice that if the knight starts on a white square, it can only go to black squares?

Jamie: Yeah, it doesn't matter how many pieces are surrounding the knight, or what size they are, it can always get out by jumping over them!

Look at this knight, surrounded by lots of enemy pieces. However, it can still move to eight squares, by jumping in the way of the arrows! It doesn't matter that all of those pieces are in the way.

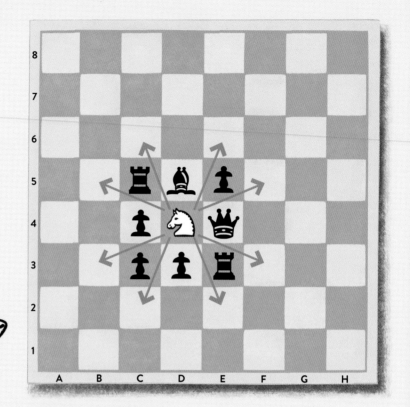

Jess: So, can the knight capture all of those pieces?

Jamie: No. In order to capture a piece, the knight must land on the piece, not just jump over it.

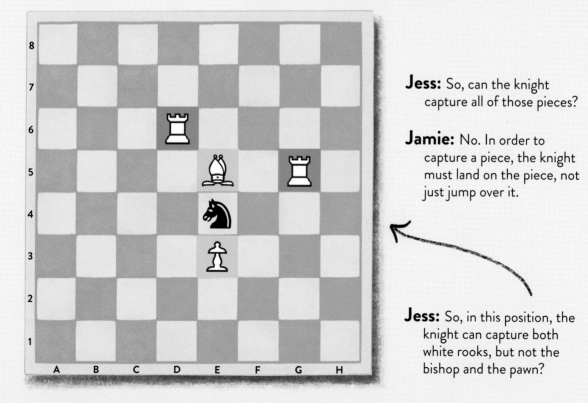

Jess: So, in this position, the knight can capture both white rooks, but not the bishop and the pawn?

Jamie: Exactly. The knight can clippety-clop its way along to both rooks, but can only jump over the bishop or the pawn.

Jess: Cool! Just like a horse.

Jamie: But it's *not* a horse! We must remember this. The knight is a special soldier, usually covered in armour. He's a brave warrior and often fights on a horse. So he's the man riding the horse, not the horse itself!

Jess: OK, I understand. I suppose you wouldn't want just a horse fighting in a battle, you would want the brave soldier. Just *one* knight seems very complicated, and we have two of them each!

Hungry Horses

Jamie: I think there are loads of games we can play to practise the knight moves. Since it's the most complicated piece, I think we need the most practice with it.

Jess: I agree. My favourite game, though, is **Hungry Horse**.

Jamie: Which one is that?

Jess: The one where both teams have all the pieces we've learnt so far in their starting positions, but the opponent has their knight in the middle of our pieces! The aim of the game is to eat all of our opponent's pieces, before they eat ours! We can't move any of our pieces, just our knights.

Jamie: Cool! But won't we need three knights each if we do that? Don't we only have two knights each?

Jess: Well noticed, Jamie! We each only have one knight that needs to be eaten. We can choose which knight that is.

Jamie: OK, so does this position look correct to start a game of Hungry Horse?

Jess: It looks great!

Jamie: I know another game, but it's an individual challenge.

Jess: What is it?

Jamie: I call it the **Knight Hop**. We have one knight, which starts on a1, but we must hop it to every corner of the board and back to its original square.

Jess: That sounds easy!

Jamie: Ah, but we have to do it in order – a1, h1, h8, a8 and then a1 again. Plus there are obstacles on the board. Look:

The knight can't land on any pawns, nor can it land on any squares where the pawns attack. Remember, the black pawns go down the board, so the pawn on c3 attacks the squares b2 and d2.

Jess: Ooh, that makes it a lot more difficult. But I like games we can play against each other!

Jamie: We can still make it competitive. We can time each other to see who does it the quickest, or we can see who does it in the smallest number of moves.

Jess: Good idea! Let's do it!

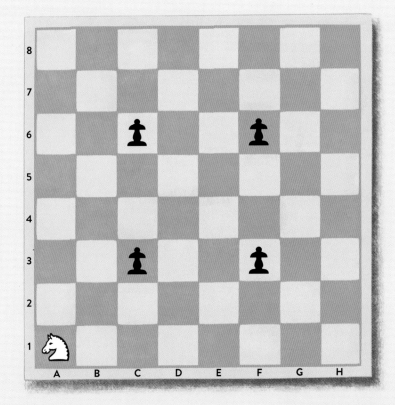

The King

Jamie: The king is the most important piece on the board, no matter what anyone says. He's the one whom we must take care of the most.

Jess: Yeah, because if he gets trapped, then we lose the game. We'll tell you more about that later.

Jamie: The king is a really old man and he can't walk very far. So we must look after him, because if there's any danger nearby, he can't run away – he only shuffles very slowly.

Jess: He's flexible, however, and can move in any direction, but just one square at a time.

Jamie: The king can never, ever be captured though – this is against the rules. As soon as the king is in danger, we *must* move him to safety. The king remains on the board at all times.

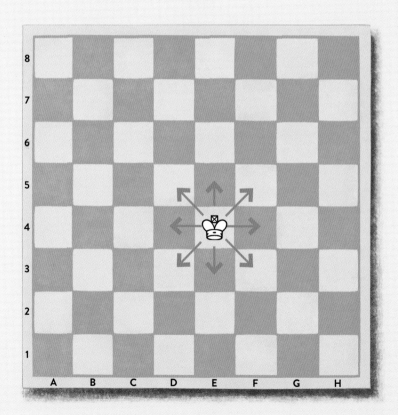

Jess: If we notice another piece is controlling the square that our king wants to go to, we can't move to that square. Instead, we must choose another square. One that is safe.

Jamie: For example, in this diagram, the white king is struggling to find a safe square to move to:

The squares d3, d4 and d5 are being attacked by the black rook, so the white king can't go to those squares. The squares b3, b4, b5 and c5 are being attacked by the black queen, so the white king can't go to those squares either. However, c3 is not being attacked by any opposing pieces, so the white king can safely move to this square.

Jess: This is one of the most important rules to understand about the king, and often it's the one that takes the longest to master.

Jamie: We must also remember that the opposing kings can NEVER go next to each other! They hate each other, and will just quarrel non-stop if they go that close to each other.

Jess: Yes, so make sure you leave at least one square in between them at all times.

Jamie: Sometimes I get a bit confused between the king and the queen.

Jess: Well, I look at their crowns; the king's crown always has a cross on it.

Mine Alert

Jamie: I have another individual challenge to practise the king movement and make sure that it never goes into danger.

Jess: What is it?

Jamie: It's called **Mine Alert**. The challenge is to move the king to a particular square safely, one step at a time. However, there are pieces from the opposing teams who are mines. You can't step on a mine, nor step on a square that's being controlled by a mine, or the king will be blown up! You must reach the target square *safely*.

Jess: Sounds dangerous!

Jamie: It is, so be careful! We can time each other to see who finds the safe route the quickest. Here is an example of a Mine Alert puzzle:

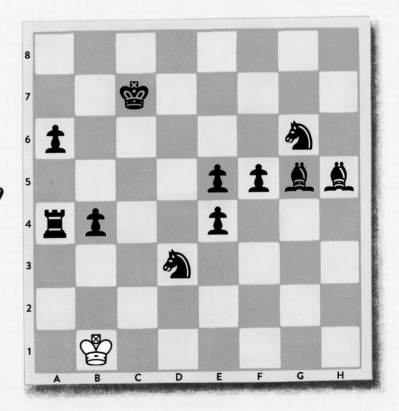

In this one, you must move the white king to e8 safely.

Jess: I may make my own Mine Alert puzzles – they look fun.

Trying to Kill the King

Jamie: Now we know all about what the king does and how important he is, we'll learn about how to kill him!

However, we have discovered that the king can never be taken off the board. So how exactly do we kill him? First of all, we need to learn how to threaten him.

The white queen is *checking* the black king.

The black rook is *checking* the white king.

The white bishop is *checking* the black king.

The black knight is *checking* the white king.

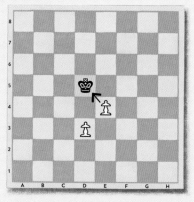

The white pawn is *checking* the black king.

Jess: Did you know that when you attack the king, it has a special name?

Jamie: Yeah, it's called The King Killer!

Jess: No, it's not! It's called **check**. Any piece apart from the king can check another king. Look at these positions:

Jamie: Ah, but in that last picture, the black king can take the white pawn! So that's not really check!

Jess: Actually, the king can't take the pawn, because White has another pawn protecting it. The pawn on d3 prevents the black king capturing the pawn on e4. Remember, the king can never put himself in danger, so he's not allowed to move to a square where he's being attacked! Also, it is still check.

Jamie: So what's the big deal then with this checking business? I can just ignore it and carry on with my own plan, since you can't capture my king, remember!

Jess: You can't do that. When you are in check, you must move *immediately* out of check to a safe place, otherwise you are leaving your king in danger.

Jamie: So when someone checks the king, does that mean they have won, because they are threatening to kill the king?

Jess: No, they don't win unless the king can't get out of the check. However, there are three different ways to get out of check. I like to remember them like the alphabet!

A – **A**void the check: run away with the king.

B – **B**lock the check: put another piece in between the attacker and your king.

C – **C**apture the piece that is checking you. You do not have to capture the piece with the king – it can be with any of your own pieces. If your opponent's piece has been captured, it can no longer be checking your king!

Look at the position below. There are many ways for Black to get out of check – which do you think is the best?

Jamie: Well, the black king is danger so I must move him immediately. The only safe square to move him to is e7, since the kings can't go next to each other.

Jess: Well, that's kinda right, Jamie. That is the only safe square for the king, but remember the **ABC**! There are other options that you haven't explored.

Jamie: Oh yeah! I totally forgot. I can do **B** – block. The rook can move from e1 all the way to e8 and block the check as the queen won't be attacking the king any more. Oh, and I have just noticed I can also do **C** – capture! There's a sneaky bishop sitting on h2 and I can move that all the way up to b8 and capture the white queen! I definitely want to do that one!

Jess: You see, always remember your ABC! There will often be more than one option.

Jamie: Wow, that's a really good way of remembering how to get out of check. It's as easy as A, B, C! Now I'll always look at all three options when I'm in check and not just move my king all the time.

Look at this position and try to do your ABCs. The black king can't move, so can't run away or avoid the check. There are no other pieces on the board, nor any room to block the check, and the queen can't be captured because the white king is protecting her. This is checkmate!

Jamie: Great! Now I know how to finish someone off. We don't try to capture the king, we must surround him and trap him so he can't escape, and that's checkmate!

But I do have a question, Jess. What happens if I can't do my ABCs, but my king is actually safe where it is?

Jess: Ah, we'll come to that later.

But Jess, what if I can't do any of those things? What if the ABC doesn't work?

Jess: Well then, Jamie, that means you are in **checkmate** and the game is over!

Getting Your King Safe

Jess: Remember we talked about how important our king is and how we must keep him safe?

Jamie: Yes...

Jess: Well, there's a special move that allows us to do this in a clever way.

Jamie: Oh yes, I've heard about this move, but I can't remember what it is!

Jess: I'll give you a clue... You get to break three rules when you do it!

1) You get to move two pieces at the same time.

2) You get to move the king two spaces.

3) The rook gets to jump over or go around the king.

Jamie: I know exactly what you are talking about now! It's called **castling**.

Jess: Exactly – it's the dance between the king and the rook.

Jamie: There are some rules for when you can and can't castle, though. First of all, there must be space between the king and the rook – no pieces can be there.

Also, neither the king nor the rook can have moved at all. So, in this position, White can castle by moving his king two squares toward his rook – to g1. Then, in the same move, the white rook can move around the king and sit on f1. This is called castling **kingside**, since the king started on this side of the board.

Black can also castle in this position, but on the other side of the board. The black king would end up on c8 after moving two squares toward the rook and the black rook will end up on d8. This is called castling **queenside**, as this is the side of the board the queen started on!

Therefore, the position will then look like this:

Jess: But why does this make our kings safer than having them where they were?

Jamie: Because usually there are other pieces on the board and it tucks our king behind a row of pawns. I'll show you – let's set up the board in the starting position.

Jess: OK. By the way, I have a great way of remembering how to do that properly.

Setting Up the Board Correctly

Jess: OK. First of all, let's look at an empty board.

Jamie: Wait a minute, Jess, there's something weird about this board...

Jess: Like what? It's just a normal board!

Jamie: It's the wrong way around!!

Jess: Ah, so it is! I didn't say the rhyme when I put it down. **White must go on the right!**

So the board should actually look like this!

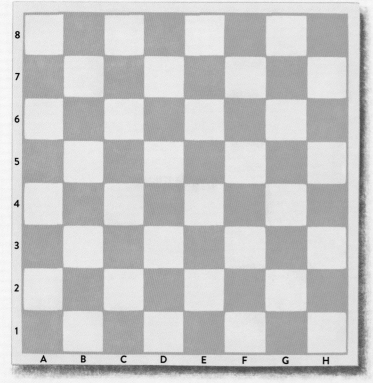

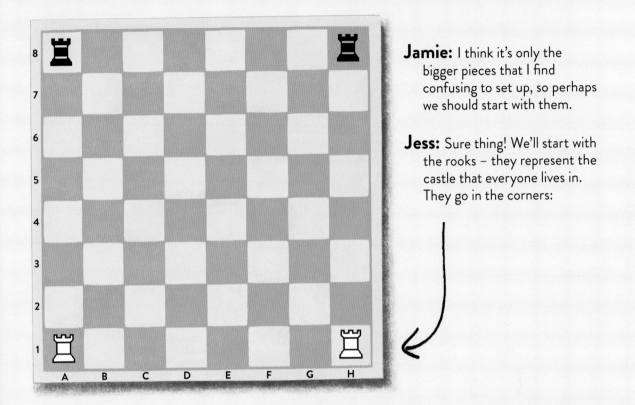

Jamie: I think it's only the bigger pieces that I find confusing to set up, so perhaps we should start with them.

Jess: Sure thing! We'll start with the rooks – they represent the castle that everyone lives in. They go in the corners:

Then, in order to protect everyone in the castle, the knights go next to the rooks.

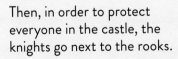

Now, the king and the queen sit on their thrones in the middle of the castle, but you have to remember which way around they go!

Jamie: I remember, you were telling me about how stylish the queen is and how she always matches her shoes and her handbag with her dress. So she must go on her own colour!

Jess: Correct, so let's put the white queen on the white throne and the black queen on the black throne. Their kings always sit next to them.

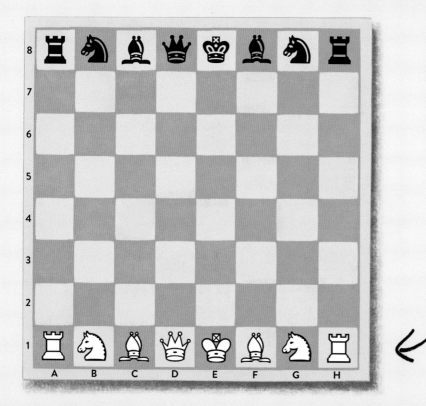

Finally, since the bishops are the king and queen's advisors, they sit next to them on the last remaining squares on the back rank.

So the big pieces are all lined up like this:

All that's left is to put on all the pawns! We should remember from page 17 that the white pawns go on the second rank and the black pawns on the seventh rank. Therefore, the final position will look like this:

Jamie: Great way of remembering it, Jess. It makes it nice and easy. The position looks just like how I set it up at the beginning of the book.

Why We Should Castle

Jamie: Remember we said that our king is the most important piece on the board? Well, this is why we castle – to try to keep him safe.

Jess: When the king stays in the centre of the board, he's more likely to get attacked, because that's where all the action takes place. The files are more likely to open up in the centre and then the opponent's pieces can start to attack. However, when the king is castled, he's nearer the edge of the board and tucked away from danger a lot more.

Jamie: In this position, I'd much rather be White. White has castled and so his king sits tucked behind three pawns that are protecting him. Black still has his king in the middle of the board, and White could now take advantage of that by advancing his pawn to d4.

Jess: Why is that good?

Jamie: Well, we'll delve more into that later. I'm talking about **tactics** and **strategy**. The fact that moving the white pawn to d4 would win some points is a tactical weapon, but castling and deciding that side of the board is the safest part of the board to put the king is **strategy**.

Jess: Cool! We sound like professional chess players now, talking about tactics and strategy! I guess good strategy would not be to move our pawns in front of our king once we've castled?!

Jamie: Exactly – they are there to protect the king and that's why we've castled, to hide behind them. So there isn't much point if we are just going to move them away.

Jess: Good strategy!

When You Can or Can't Castle

Jamie: So we mentioned that we must have space in between our king and our rook to castle.

Jess: And we must not have previously moved either of them at all!

Jamie: Yes, that too. But when are we *not* allowed to castle? There are three main important situations you must know:

1) **You can't castle when you are *in* check**
   The white king can't castle on either side of the board because he is currently in check. He must first get out of check before he can castle. However, since he can neither block the check nor capture the bishop, he must move his king. Then once he has moved his king, he can't castle!

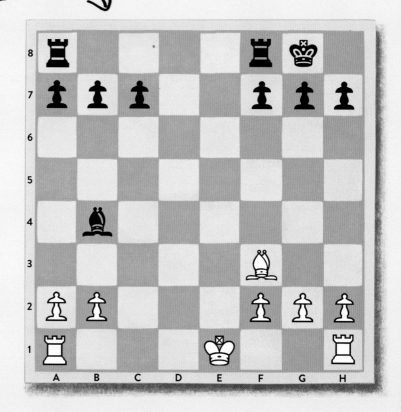

2) You can't castle *into* check

White would love to castle in this position, but the square his king would land on, g1, is being attacked by the black bishop on c5. Remember the king can never walk into danger, so he can't castle into check.

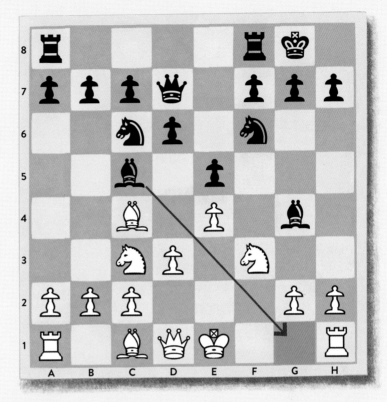

3) You can't castle *through* check

This one is a little bit more tricky, but if one of the opponent's pieces is controlling the square that the king passes through when he is trying to castle, this is still not allowed. The king will again have to walk through danger. Therefore, in this position, the white king can't castle as the black rook is covering the f1 square.

Jess: Those are a lot of rules to remember, so my advice is to castle quite soon at the beginning of the game, and that way you won't have to worry about getting checked!

Pawn Magic

Jamie: Why are we back to learning about pawns again? We've already done the pawns and they can't even go backward. I don't like them!

Jess: But we haven't learnt everything about them – there are some pretty special moves they can make, you know.

Jamie: Really? Like what? Move backward?

Jess: No, not move backward, you know that. But they can do magic!

Jamie: Ooh, I like magic! What can they do?

Jess: First of all, there's a special move in which pawns can take other pawns in a strange way. If you haven't seen it before, it may look like cheating!

Jamie: How does it work?

Jess: Take a look at the position below:

There's only one pawn on the board right now who can create some magic – the pawn on d5. This is because, in order to do the magic, the pawn must be on the *5th rank*.

Jamie: But the pawn on c5 is on the 5th rank too...

Jess: Ah, but I mean *their* 5th rank. The black pawn on c5 is only on Black's 4th rank. It may be on the rank that says number 5, but it's not *Black's* 5th rank.

Jamie: Oh, I get it. So what's it allowed to do when it reaches the 5th rank?

Jess: Well, as a reward for getting just past halfway, it obtains an extra power. If an opposing pawn tries to go past him by moving two squares, then he can capture that pawn as if it only went one square. So if the black pawn on e7 were to move to e5 in one go, the white pawn can catch him!

Jamie: No way!

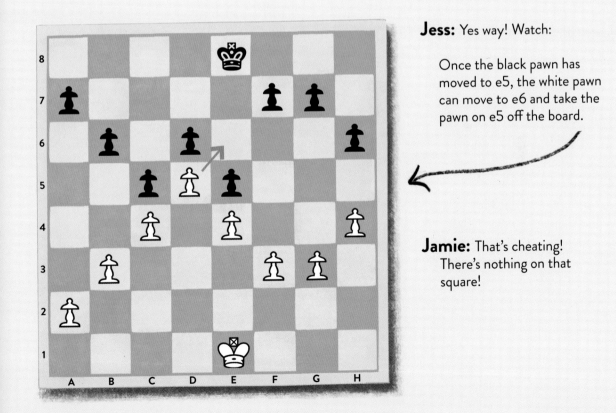

Jess: Yes way! Watch:

Once the black pawn has moved to e5, the white pawn can move to e6 and take the pawn on e5 off the board.

Jamie: That's cheating! There's nothing on that square!

Jess: I told you it looks like cheating, but it isn't. It's called **en passant**.

Jamie: That's not even English!

Jess: I know; it's French. It means 'in passing'. So as the pawn passes by the one on the 5th rank, then en passant is an option.

However, the en passant capture must be made immediately. If you choose to make another move first, you can no longer take en passant.

Jamie: Well, that's useful to know. What about the pawn on c5? Could that not have been taken by en passant in the first place?

Jess: Well, it's Black to play in that position, and the en passant capture can only be made if it's immediately after the pawn moves two squares.

Jamie: I see. So let me get this right, to capture en passant:

1) Our pawn must be on our 5th rank.

2) The opposing pawn must be on the file next to our pawn and on its starting square, and then move two squares forward, so it's next to our pawn.

3) Then, if we decide to capture the pawn, we must do so as if it had only moved one square, so we're still going diagonally, but just not landing on the square the pawn is on.

4) We must do this immediately after the opposing pawn has moved two squares forward, otherwise our chance is gone.

Jess: Exactly! Well done!

Jamie: My head hurts...

Jess: It *is* a tricky one. Let's do an exercise to see if you really have got it.

Jamie, can anyone capture en passant here?

Jamie: Well, that's a trick question. It depends on whose move it is and what the last move played was!

Jess: Well noticed. So if it's Black to play and the last move played was the white pawn from g2 to g4?

Jamie: Then the pawn on h4 can capture it en passant.

Jess: Well done! Which other of Black's pawns are waiting to do en passant?

Jamie: The one on d4. If either the pawn on c2 or e2 moves two squares forward, it can get them!

Jess: I think you've got it – great, we can move on!

Jamie: Oh, what's next?

Jess: Pawn Promotion.

Jamie: Ah, promotion. That's like getting an upgrade in a job, right?

Jess: Yeah, it's like that. Promotion is advancement in a rank or position.

Jamie: So a pawn can get promoted? When?

Jess: When he gets to the end of the board. As a reward for making it safely past all of the enemy's pieces and getting to his first rank, he can promote to a piece of a higher value.

Jamie: I'd choose a king, because he's the most important!

Jess: Ah, but they can't promote to a king. They can choose between a queen, rook, bishop or knight.

Jamie: Cool! So does the pawn drink some Polyjuice Potion when he gets to the end of the board or something?

Jess: Enough with the Harry Potter! He just gets to choose what he would like to become, and then that piece is put on the board in place of the promoted pawn.

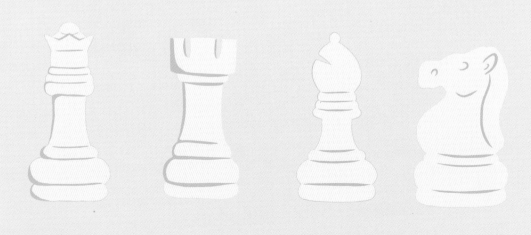

Jamie: I'd then choose a queen because she can do the most! Why would anyone choose any of the other pieces?

Jess: Because sometimes it's bad to choose a queen – I'll give you an example later. Or sometimes you want a knight, because nothing else moves like it and you could use it to trick your opponent.

Jamie: But that must almost never happen, though, right?

Jess: It's rare, but it can happen. It's called **under-promotion** because you are not promoting to the highest value you can.

Jamie: Value?

Jess: Yes, we mentioned that pawns are worth one point on page 16. Let's talk some more about the values.

Scoring Points

Jamie: I thought that there wasn't a scoring system in chess? I thought that you could only win by giving checkmate.

Jess: There isn't, but we attach values to each of the pieces to help guide us through the game, so we can see which ones are stronger and who is winning.

Jamie: Ah yes, I think of them in terms of money! Like a pawn is worth one pound, or one dollar.

Jess: I just use points, but whatever works for you!

You can think of them in terms of points or as pounds or dollars!

Jamie: What about the king?

Jess: Well, we can't capture the king, can we? So therefore we can't give him any points value, but perhaps we can say the king is worth the whole game!

Jamie: Good idea. So now that I have all the values here, I can see who is winning in our match at the moment. What have you taken at the moment Jess?

Jess: I have taken a queen, a rook and a pawn. What about you?

Jamie: Well I have taken a queen, two knights, a bishop and two pawns.

= 1 point   = 3 points   = 3 points   = 5 points   = 9 points

Jess: Let's add them up! My  + + = 15 points.

Jamie: My + + + + + = 20 points.

So I'm winning. Ha ha!

Jess: OK, no need for that. I think we need to discuss chess etiquette!

Jamie: OK...

Playtime!

Jamie: I think we're ready for a game now! I know all the rules.

Jess: Do you?! Go on... Prove it!

Jamie: OK, so I know the names of all the pieces and how they move.

I know that the pawn doesn't ever move backward but has two special powers – en passant and promotion. It's also worth one point.

I know that a knight is the only piece that can jump and no other piece moves in an L-shape as it does. It's worth three points.

I know that the bishop is worth the same amount of points as the knight because it can move further, but is restricted to squares of one colour on the board.

The rook is worth five points and it can move up and down and across the board in straight lines.

The queen is the most powerful and she can travel in every direction, apart from the way a knight moves. She's worth nine points.

Then the king can go in any direction, but only one square at a time because he is old. He is the most important, though, and we must try to keep him safe at all times. He doesn't have a points value because he can never be captured.

Jess: Wow! That's a lot you've remembered.

Jamie: Wait, there's more!

When the king is attacked, it's called **check**, and he has three types of ways to get out of it: he can avoid the check, block the check or capture the piece that's checking him. If he can't do any of these things and is still in danger, then he is in **checkmate** and that means the game is over.

To try and keep our king safe, we have another special move called **castling**, which is when the king moves two squares toward the rook and then the rook jumps over the king. We do this because usually we have pawns in front of our king to protect it then. However, we can't castle into check, out of check or through check.

Jess: OK, OK, stop showing off now. You know everything!

Jamie: OK, so let's play a game.

Jess: First of all, I'd like to talk to you about your behaviour! You should behave in a certain way when you play chess. As I've already mentioned, it's called **chess etiquette**.

Chess Etiquette

Jamie: What on earth does 'etiquette' mean? Is it a dance? We don't have to dance when we play chess, do we? If so, I don't want to play!

Jess: Of course we don't have to dance. 'Etiquette' means 'good behaviour' – something YOU need to learn, Jamie!

First of all, before we start the game, we need to shake hands. This shows we have good sportsmanship and wish each other a good game.

Jamie: No problem, good luck Jess. You're gonna need it!

The Top Five Rules of Chess Etiquette

1. Before you start a game of chess, shake hands with your opponent and say 'good luck' to them. This shows good sportsmanship.

2. Chess is a quiet game, so you should be sitting quietly and thinking during the game, not shouting or talking or doing anything to put your opponent off.

3. Always observe the 'touch-move' rule and the 'touch-take' rule: see opposite page.

4. At the end of the game, shake hands with your opponent again and say 'well done', regardless of the result.

5. Once you've finished the game, set up the board in the starting position. This will ensure that you haven't lost any of the pieces, and the board will be ready for the next match!

Jess: And things like that, Jamie! No snide remarks. Chess is known as the royal game, you know, so start being better-behaved!

Jamie: OK, well, then I'm going to invoke tournament rules. **TOUCH MOVE!**

Jess: What??

Jamie: If you touch a piece, you *have* to move it, even if you don't want to. Those are the professional rules. So that means you have to think about your moves first to make sure you definitely want to move the piece you touch!

Jess: OK, fine, I suppose that includes **touch take**, too?

Jamie: Yes, Jess. If you touch one of my pieces and you can take it, you must do so. So come on, I want to play so I can beat you and show you who's boss!

Jess: See what I mean, Jamie? That's not very good chess etiquette. I don't want to see you showing off if you do win.

Jamie: You know that there's not always a winner and loser in chess?

Jess: Of course. Sometimes neither of us can win and the game ends up in a draw. Let's see how.

Ways to Draw

Jamie: Most people have heard of a type of draw in chess called **stalemate** and think that every type of draw is called stalemate, but it isn't! Stalemate actually refers to a very particular type of position.

Jess: Yes, very specific. We sort of mentioned it earlier, but I didn't tell you much about it.

When you have a situation where you think you are in checkmate because your king can't go anywhere safe, but your king is actually safe on the square where it's sitting; this is called **stalemate**.

Take a look at the position below:

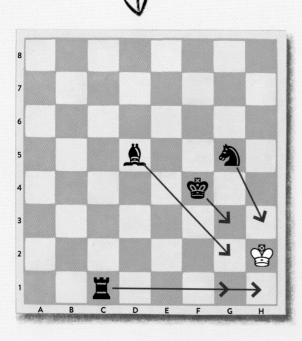

Here, the king can't move anywhere because the black pieces are covering all the squares around him and he can't move into danger. However, do you notice that the king is completely safe where he is? No one is attacking him on that square, so why can't he just stay there?

Jamie: Exactly. **Checkmate** is only if you've trapped the king but are threatening him at the same time. Otherwise it's stalemate.

Jess: And this doesn't mean you win! You must checkmate to win. Stalemate is only a draw. So if you are the one with lots of pieces, this isn't good for you, because you'll deprive yourself of the full points you could have had if you had won. However, if you are the one with just the king, then well done! This is great news for you.

Jamie: A good tip, I think, when I'm winning by lots and trying to avoid stalemate, is to try to check all the time. That way, I know that if the king does run out of squares, it will be checkmate and not stalemate.

Jess: Ah, but don't just keep checking with the same piece, otherwise this may also end in another type of draw. Try to use lots of different pieces – it'll make it easier to cover more squares.

Jamie: What other type of draw do you mean?

Jess: Well, there's a draw called a **3-fold repetition**. It's rather a confusing type of draw and many people often get it wrong. Basically, if a position is repeated three times during a game, then the game is drawn.

Jamie: That sounds easy to me!

Jess: I'm not finished! I don't just mean the same three moves in a row, but I mean it's also a draw when the exact same position, with the same player to move, occurs at any three moments in the game. So you have to remember every position in order to tell if the exact position has occurred before!

Jamie: OK, that sounds mega-complicated!

Jess: It is! Although, usually the positions will have occurred very close to each other, which is why most of the time, it happens when the same moves have been repeated three times in a row.

Jamie: Ah OK, I thought it was just a draw whenever someone moves the same move three times in a row, and it doesn't really matter what the opponent does.

Jess: No! That's what so many people think. But think about it; if that was the case, then anyone could get a draw. No one would ever lose!

Another draw could occur by checking a lot – **perpetual check**. This is when one side constantly checks the other side and the defender can never stop the checks. This could go on forever, so it's declared a draw.

Jamie: Oh yeah!! So what other draws are there?

Jess: Well, what about when there are just bare kings?

Jamie: Bare kings? That sounds naughty! Why haven't they got any clothes on?!

Jess: Jamie, no! I don't mean that! I mean that's what you say when there's only a pair of kings left on the board! Like this:

Jamie: Oh, I see! Yes, that makes sense. Since the kings can't move next to each other and there are no other pieces, then, of course, checkmate can't happen.

Jess: Exactly. So if this happens, the game is a draw.

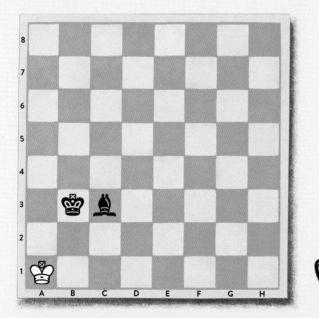

Jamie: Sometimes there may be another piece on the board with the kings, but it's still a draw.

Jess: Yeah, like if one side just had a bishop or knight. You can't checkmate with just one bishop or just one knight.

Look at this position. It's almost checkmate, but the white king can move to b1. No matter how hard I try, I can't trap the king properly with only one bishop.

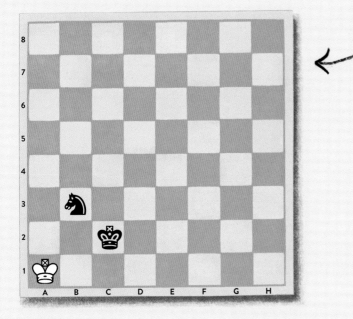

Jamie: It's the same with just one knight, too. Look!

When this happens, it's said that there's **insufficient material** to checkmate.

Jess: So, if we only have a pawn left, then that would be insufficient material. Right?!

Jamie: Wrong! That pawn can get to the end of the board and create some magic in the form of promotion and turn into a queen or a rook, which can checkmate!

Jess: Good point! So what else counts as insufficient material?

Jamie: Well, the tricky one is if you have two knights against a king.

Jess: Why is that tricky? I bet I can set up a checkmate with two knights.

See – I did it. It's checkmate. That wasn't tricky at all.

Jamie: Yes, but the difficulty is that you can't **force** your opponent into that position. They can keep their king out of the corner, and you'll never be able to get the checkmate without them letting you.

Jess: Oh, that's really annoying! So does that count as insufficient material?

Jamie: Well it isn't a draw by insufficient material, because two knights are sufficient!

Jess: Then how does it become a draw?

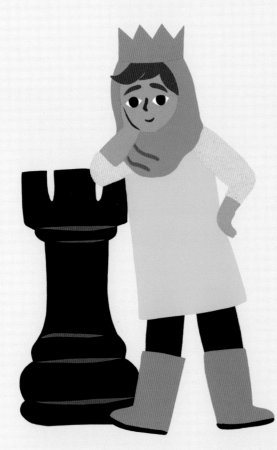

Jamie: Because no matter how hard the side with the two knights tries, they won't be able to get checkmate unless the other side *wants* to lose.

Jess: I still don't get why it's a draw. Can't they just keep playing forever and ever?

Jamie: No, because of the **50-move rule**.

Jess: What on earth is that? It sounds made up!

Jamie: No, of course not! It's the rule that prevents games going on forever and ever. It can be applied when each player has made 50 moves without a pawn move or any capture taking place. The game is then considered a draw.

Jess: I suppose that would stop people moving around all day aimlessly!

Jamie: Exactly. So it's all the more reason why you should learn how to checkmate properly, as you only have a certain amount of moves to do it in.

Jess: OK, we should make sure we cover that later in the book, then! However, all of these draws are tiring. Did you know there's a quicker way to draw?

Jamie: Oh? What's that?

Jess: You can just offer your opponent a draw!

Jamie: Of course! Yes, that's definitely the quickest way. If they accept, of course!

Jess: That's true. They might say no if they think they are winning and then the game has to go on.

Jamie: Well, I think we've learnt a lot, Jess, and we pretty much have gone over everything there is to know about chess!

Jess: Definitely. Now we can play a good game.

Jamie: In the next part of the book, we can start talking about tournaments and competitive play – my favourite!

Jess: Good idea. We can show all the tricks you need to play in competition.

Jamie: Yay!!

Chess Tournaments

Jess: Going to your first chess tournament is quite a scary experience. It's totally different from playing against your parents or friends at school.

Jamie: Yeah, all the children want to win, and you have no idea how good they are!

Jess: Some have been playing for ages and have already won lots of prizes.

Jamie: Some have chess coaches who go with them and are super serious.

Jess: And some are really mean to girls.

Jamie: Aw, I'm sorry Jess. Sometimes boys are mean.

Jess: Yeah, they are!

Jamie: Well, let's make sure that we pass on our advice on how to deal with the meanies, and show some really cool tricks with things we've picked up from our tournaments.

Jess: Tournaments are super fun if you go prepared.

Jamie: You get to win some really awesome trophies!

Jess: And sometimes money!

Jamie: I LOVE CHESS TOURNAMENTS!

Jess: Me too! Let's show them what we've learnt.

Tournament Play

Jess: I remember my first chess tournament. It was really scary!

Jamie: Why?

Jess: Well, I didn't know where anything was or what was going on. It was just filled with people I didn't know, and I lost loads of games!

Jamie: That sounds like most people's first tournament. They can be extremely daunting. I think the best thing to do is just try to enjoy yourself and have fun.

Jess: I wish you could have told me that before I actually played my first tournament! How did you find your first one, Jamie?

Jamie: Mine was awesome! I won most of my games and the other kids cried when I beat them! Plus, they didn't even notice when I took their pieces off the board and hid them!

Jess: WHAT? You can't do that!

Jamie: Why not?!

Jess: That's not good chess etiquette!

Jamie: Oh yeah... you and your chess etiquette.

Jess: Well, you need to behave a certain way. You can't try to put off your opponent in any sort of way. Imagine if I was pulling faces at you...would you be able to concentrate?

You definitely can't take your opponent's pieces off the board. That's cheating!

Jamie: Oh.

Jess: Yes, so I hope I don't see you doing that again.

Jamie: Well, they should have just ignored me or call the arbiter.

Jess: But it was probably their first tournament, too, and they weren't told what to do.

Jamie: Well, my advice is, if anyone is putting you off in a tournament or there's something that you are unsure of, you should put your hand up immediately and call an arbiter over. They will be able to help you.

Jess: That's good advice. There should always be adults around. Ask them to watch the game if you like. Or if you ever need to check any rules, just ask them.

Jamie: I think someone was cheating against me with the timer thingy.

Jess: You mean the chess clock?

Jamie: Yeah, they were messing about with it, always had their hand on it or behind it.

Jess: Ooh, that sounds dodgy. That shouldn't happen! Definitely call the arbiter for that.

Jamie: Aren't there rules for how to use the chess clock?

Jess: Of course. You shouldn't be touching the clock at all unless you are pressing it, which you must do with the hand that you used to move your piece.

Jamie: So, if I move the pieces with my right hand, I must press the clock with my right hand?

Jess: Yes, exactly. You can't keep your hand on the clock after that. So both players can't be touching the clock at the same time.

Jamie: I find the clock rather tricky to use. I don't know when I'm nearly out of time.

Jess: You can tell when the little flag on the clock starts to stand upright.

Jamie: Oh yes, of course. I usually think while my opponent is thinking, so I don't run out of time.

Jess: That's a good plan. If you make sure you are concentrating just as hard while it's your opponent's turn, then you won't use up as much of your own time.

Jamie: Yes, it's all part of **chess strategy** again.

Jess: My piece of advice is that every time you play in a chess tournament, you should learn from your mistakes. Don't take every loss as a disaster. Yes, it's upsetting when you lose, but it means you have so much more to learn from.

Jamie: But I don't like losing!

Jess: I know. No one does. However, if we realize that losing actually helps our chess, then we'll become much better players because of it.

Jamie: OK. I believe you...

Chess Language

Jess: Remember at the very beginning of the book, on page 10, we looked at chess notation and the language that chess players speak in?

Jamie: Of course, using co-ordinates.

Jess: Well, I think we should go over that again and explain properly how we actually write down a full chess game.

Jamie: OK, sure. I remember talking about ranks, files, diagonals and the postcodes for each square.

Jess: Yes, but when we are writing down a chess game, we need a sort of code to show which moves we mean.

Jamie: But what's the point of notating?

Jess: There are so many reasons! First of all, if we want to know what on earth chess professionals are on about when they're blabbering on in chess language, then we need to understand chess notation.

Then, there are times where you may get a dishonest opponent and they may cheat. A bit like you did before, Jamie!

Jamie: Oi! I feel bad about that already.

Jess: Well, it also might be innocent – you may forget whose move it is or where the pieces were.

Jamie: These sound like good enough reasons to me.

Jess: Well, each of the pieces is assigned a letter so we know which ones move on each turn. These should be easy to remember:

Rook = **R**
Bishop = **B**
Queen = **Q**
King = **K**
Knight = **N**

1. e4 e5
2. Nf3 d6
3. d4 Bg4
4. dxe5 Bxf3

Jamie: OK, that seems easy enough, but two things; why is the knight given an N? It starts with a silent K, remember? Also, you didn't mention the pawn.

Jess: Good questions! Well, we've already used a K for the king, so it would be confusing to have two pieces with the same letter.

Jamie: Then why not Kn?

Jess: Because that's two letters! It's much easier to just use N. And for pawn moves, only the co-ordinates of the squares are used.

Jamie: That makes sense. I want to learn what to write if I want to comment on games.

Jess: Well, these notations are mainly found in books. We don't need to write them down when we play our own games. There are also symbols, so we know what the authors and commentators think about the moves. For example, the main symbols used are:

Good move = !
Bad move = ?
Excellent move = !!
Blunder = ??
Interesting move = !?
Dubious move = ?!

Jamie: What do we mean by blunder or dubious?

Jess: A blunder is a move that gives away material or allows something bad to happen in the position. A dubious move is one that just looks a bit iffy! It may not blunder any pieces as such, but is probably not appropriate for the position.

Jamie: Oh, I see – a lot of my moves are dubious! Well, how about evaluating the position? What are the symbols for that?

Jess: Well, these symbols are extremely important because, these days, computers are a big part of chess. Computers use symbols to represent who they think is better in each position. These include:

White is slightly better   +/=
Black is slightly better   =/+
White is better   +/-
Black is better   -/+
White is winning   +-
Black is winning   -+
Equal   =
Unclear   ∞
With compensation   =/∞

Jamie: What does 'compensation' mean?

Jess: It's when you are material down, usually a pawn or two, but you have a good position and can do lots of good things. We say that you have compensation for the material lost.

Jamie: This is brilliant. Now I can read loads of chess books and magazines and get really, really good at chess!

Getting Off to a Good Start

Jamie: When I play chess, I like to start off really well as it gives a good impression of myself as a player.

Jess: Me too! There are three main stages of the game: **opening**, **middlegame** and **ending**. We'll give you tips on all of the important aspects of each stage of the game.

Jamie: Let's start with the opening. I have a few ideas of what I always do at the beginning of the game.

First of all, I like to take control of the centre. I usually do this by putting the pawn in front of my king up two squares. If my opponent lets me, I'll put the other middle pawn up two squares as well!

Jess: If you control the centre, you control the game. That's my motto! The centre is where all the action happens.

Jamie: I then bring out my minor pieces toward the centre, too.

Jess: What do you mean by **minor** pieces? Are they sad? Like in music, when a minor key sounds sad?

Jamie: No, I mean that minor pieces are the knights and the bishops, since they are not worth as much, and the major pieces are the rooks and queen.

Jess: OK, that makes sense.

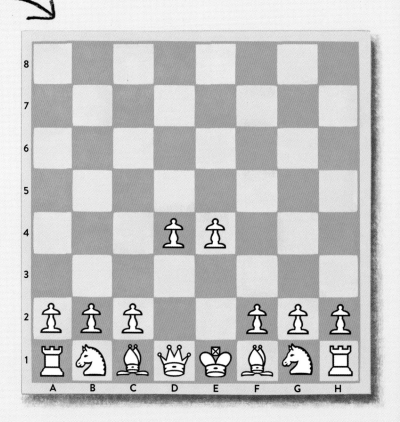

Jamie: So I get the minor pieces out first and direct them all toward the centre, so they look a bit like this:

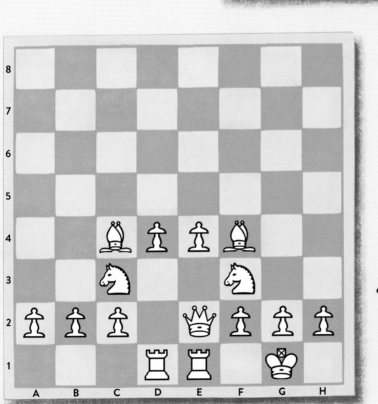

Jess: Cool! You are controlling so many squares!!

Jamie: That's the point! Now I just need to make sure that I get my king safe.

Jess: You need to castle!!

Jamie: Exactly. I'll castle, and also connect my rooks.

Jess: Connect your rooks?

Jamie: Yes, I clear the path between them so they defend each other. I do that and then put them pointing toward the centre, too. The ideal position looks like this:

Jess: That setup looks so cool! Like some kind of perfectly placed army ready to charge at you.

Jamie: That's why it's called a **Bull's Head**. The way the pieces are arranged, it looks like a bull's head! Sometimes, the bishops are on b5 and g5 instead.

Jess: But no one is going to let you do all that! They're going to try to stop you setting up the Bull's Head and try to do it themselves.

Jamie: That's why the opening is like a race to get your pieces out as quickly as possible. If you don't, your opponent will just take all the good squares.

Jess: It's like they're on starting blocks and they're desperate to get off them.

Jamie: Well, however you remember it, you must realize that whoever has the best start to the game is going to have more chances throughout the middlegame.

Chess Maths

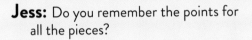

Jess: Do you remember the points for all the pieces?

Jamie: Of course. The pawn is worth 1 point, the knight and the bishop are worth 3 points each, the rook is 5 points and the queen is 9 points.

Jess: Well done! Well, you have to remember these so you can see how you're getting on during the game. We are always doing lots of chess maths during our games.

Jamie: I love capturing pieces. I take the opponent's pieces and make a little prison for them by my side of the board.

Jess: Well, you hardly get to take any of mine, because I don't leave my pieces **undefended**.

Jamie: What do you mean?

Jess: Well, all my pieces are always backed up by other members of my team. This way, if any opponents attack my pieces, they won't win anything. I always remember that **every tactic comes from an undefended piece.**

Jamie: What do you mean by tactic?

Jess: It's like a trick. We'll talk about it later.

Jamie: One of the tips I think of when I'm looking for captures is that I always look out for undefended pieces and capture those because they are **free pieces**. You gain lots of points, and they don't gain any. So when you see a piece looking a bit lost and alone, nab it!

Jess: Sometimes you can capture a piece and it's not undefended, so they can capture you back. This can be OK as long as they are capturing a piece that's worth the same amount of points or less than the one you captured!

Jamie: OK, I think I get it. So if I can capture a bishop, if they can capture a bishop or knight back, then this will be equal.

Jess: Exactly, this will be called an **exchange**.

Jamie: What if I captured a bishop and they only captured a pawn?

Jess: Then this will be called an **advantageous exchange** for you.

Jamie: Because I win 3 points and they would only win 1 point?

Jess: Yes. As long as you get more points from the exchange, it will be advantageous. Obviously, it's not always about the points, though, as the position is always important.

The Classic Trick

Jamie: The more chess you play, the more you realize there are some tricks that people will try to play on you. The most classic one is called **Scholar's Mate** because it's the most effective!

Jess: Is that the same as the four-move checkmate?

Jamie: Yeah, it's the same thing! We call it Scholar's Mate, because it happens to those who are still very much learning the game.

Jess: So the reason why this checkmate is so effective is because, at the beginning of the game, there's a real weak spot near the king that can be attacked quite easily. If enough pressure is piled on it, some real damage can be caused.

The weak spot is on f7:

Jamie: I call that square the **Achilles' heel** of the chessboard at the beginning of the game. White's Achilles heel is on f2.

Jess: Why Achilles' heel?

Jamie: Do you not know who Achilles is?!

Jess: He's some Greek hero is all I know!

Jamie: He was one of the greatest fighters ever! He was immortal – could live forever – because his mum dipped him in a river of immortality when he was a baby. However, she held him by his heel, so that part of him was not dipped in, and therefore became the only part of him that could get injured – it was his weak spot.

Jess: I see the comparison! The chess army is strong overall, but at the beginning, f2 and f7 are weak, just like Achilles' heel.

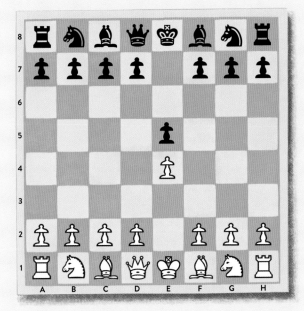

Jamie: Yes! That's how he died – he got shot in the heel during a battle. It was very sad.

Jess: I suppose when something is weak, the enemy will aim for it.

Jamie: Well, that's what they do in Scholar's Mate – they gang up on f7 with the queen and the bishop.

Jess: Why do you think people fall for it so often?

Jamie: Because it's very easy to! You don't really have to make any bad moves. Your moves can still look like good moves, but you just get checkmated!

Jess: I gotta see this now!

Jamie: So usually, things start off like this:

Jess: Both sides are trying to get control of the centre. It makes sense!

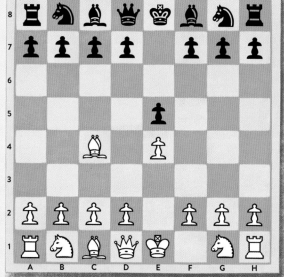

Jamie: Yes. Next, we both try to get our minor pieces out, directing them toward the centre.

Jess: KNIGHTS ON THE RIM ARE DIM!

Jamie: Huh?!

Jess: That's the clever phrase to help remember that we should always put our knights toward the centre of the board and not on the side.

Jamie: Well, that's how many good players start their game, but this is not how Scholars' Mate goes. In order to do the four-move checkmate, we bring out our bishop first, to attack the Achilles' heel.

Jess: I can see it's pointing straight at f7!

Jamie: Well, Black usually develops one of his knights here – either to c6 or to f6. I'll start with one to c6. Then White brings out his most powerful piece, his queen.

Jess: Let me guess, to f3?

Jamie: Actually, no, that's not the best square for the queen, and we'll see why in a minute. Let's put the queen on h5 instead.

Jess: Oh no, they're both pointing at the Achilles' heel! If the queen were to take the pawn on f7, that would be **checkmate!**

Jamie: Exactly! So you need to do something about that. Notice how the queen attacks h7 and e5, too, but she's not **threatening** them. It's only a **threat** when the pawn or piece can be taken safely; otherwise it's just an attack. The pawn on f7 is definitely **threatened!**

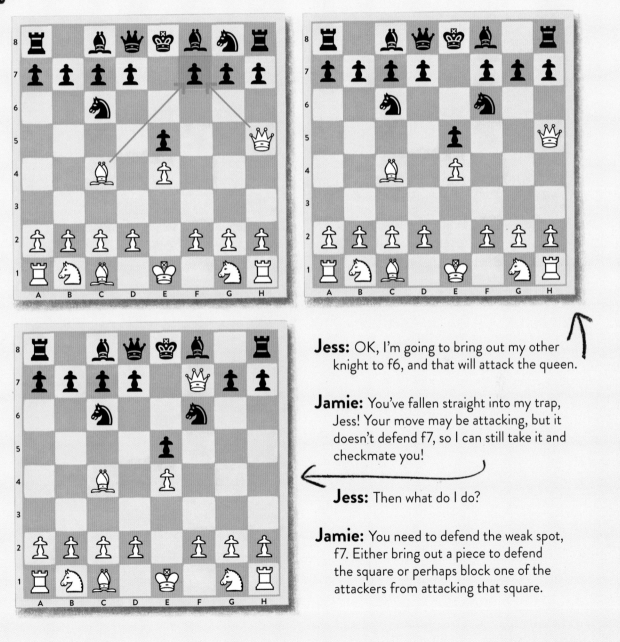

Jess: OK, I'm going to bring out my other knight to f6, and that will attack the queen.

Jamie: You've fallen straight into my trap, Jess! Your move may be attacking, but it doesn't defend f7, so I can still take it and checkmate you!

Jess: Then what do I do?

Jamie: You need to defend the weak spot, f7. Either bring out a piece to defend the square or perhaps block one of the attackers from attacking that square.

Jess: Oh, *I* know, I might move my pawn from g7 to g6. That way, it blocks the white queen from getting to f7, and also I'm attacking her. If she doesn't move out of the way, I'll capture her.

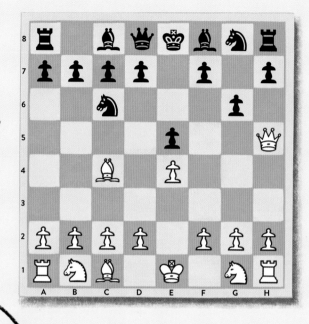

Jamie: Great plan! What if the queen now just moves back to f3?!

Jess: Oh no! She's STILL threatening my Achilles' heel and threatening checkmate! Gosh, this is very annoying!

OK, well I think the best thing to do is to get my other knight out to f6. I remember that I should be developing my pieces in the beginning of the game. Also, the knight blocks the path of the queen to my Achilles' heel, so I don't need to worry about checkmate for the time being.

Jamie: Good idea. I suggest you castle as soon as you can, too, to ensure that your king remains safe!

Jess: That queen and the bishop work well together! So frustrating.

Jamie: Yes they do. They **complement** each other. They are known to work together well and sometimes they can pile up on the same diagonal and form a **battery**. This can be very dangerous.

Jess: I don't like it. I'm glad I'm more aware of it now and can stop it.

Jamie: Just watch out, though. There's another trap you can fall into. If they bring out their queen first, then you have to be a little bit careful.

Jess: Why? I can just do the same thing. Surely it doesn't matter which order they do it in.

Jamie: Sure, but watch.

Notice how this time, the e5 pawn is **threatened** because your knight is not yet on c6, so playing g6 right now would be a serious error.

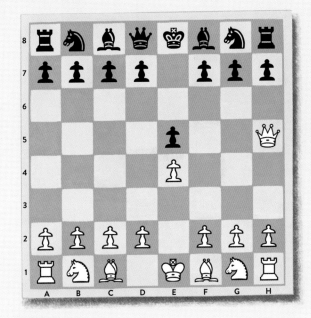

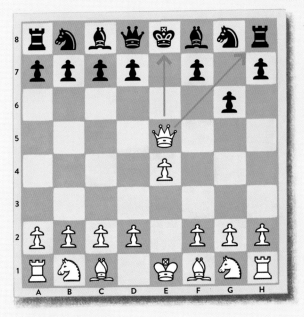

Jess: Oh I can see! You fall into a **fork**.

Jamie: A what? No, this is called a **double attack** because the queen is attacking both the king and the rook at the same time. This is super strong because, since it is **check**, the king must spend a move to defend itself and won't be able to do anything about its rook.

Jess: Jamie! A **fork** is the same thing as a **double attack** really, but it's just an easier way of saying it. It can also refer to lots of pieces. I'll explain more in the next chapter!

The Fork

Jess: So, Jamie, a **fork** can also be a double attack, but it's a type of **tactic** where one piece creates two or more threats at the same time. Therefore, the fork doesn't have to just attack two or more pieces, but may also threaten checkmate at the same time. These sorts of forks are more difficult to spot.

Jamie: I have two questions. Why is it called a fork? You don't eat with it! Also, what do you mean by **tactic**?

Jess: A **tactic** is a kind of trick that you can play in chess that helps you gain an advantage. Often, that advantage is a material one, but sometimes it may be positional. We'll discuss more tactics over the next few chapters.

This tactic is called a fork because, just as with the fork we use for eating, it has many prongs.

So, going back to the position we talked about on page 87, where Black just made a mistake by playing g6, we can see that when the white queen captures the pawn on e5, it forks the king on e8 and the rook on h8.

Jamie: It's a great move! Black has to get out of check and then White can just take the rook in the corner for free.

Jess: Did you know there are names for different types of forks?

Jamie: Ah yes, I know some. I'll show you!

Look at this position. I know this can't really happen.

Black's knight is attacking both the white king and queen. When these two pieces are attacked at the same time, it's known as a **royal fork**, because it's the royal family that's being attacked. Then also, White's knight is attacking the black king, queen, AND rook! This is known as a **family fork**, because it's attacking three of the chessmen at the same time!

Jess: I love forks! They come up all the time in games, and every piece can do forks.

Jamie: Every piece?

Jess: Yes, even the king!

Jamie: Wow! Maybe we should test ourselves to see if we can fork with every piece.

Jess: Yes, that's a good exercise. Let's go do that now!

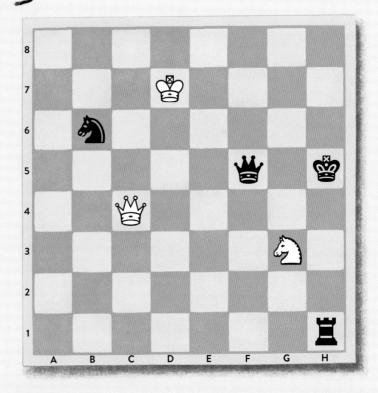

The Pin

Jamie: Now let's talk about one of my favourite types of tactic: the **pin!**

Jess: What was the pin again?

Jamie: A **pin** is a tactical device that stops an enemy piece from moving. When that piece is pinned, it loses its attacking and defending power and is rendered almost useless.

Jess: Ah, it's a bit like what a pin does in real life. I use pins to keep my posters in place on my wall. It stops them from moving!

Jamie: Yes, exactly. However, there are two different types of pin. The pin that stops the piece from moving completely is called an **absolute pin**. Look:

Jess: I see – because the knight **absolutely** can't move! It would be illegal if it moved.

Jamie: Yes, exactly. The other type of pin is called a **relative** pin because the piece can move, but it would be a bad idea if it did. Look:

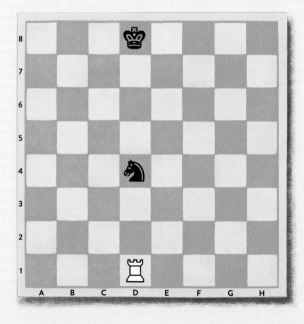

Jess: OK, so the knight *can* move, but if it did, the queen would be taken. So it is **relatively** pinned. I get it!

Jamie: Unlike the fork, only three pieces can pin – the queen, rook and bishop.

Jess: They are the **line pieces**!

Jamie: Yes, exactly, so they can pin because they control the whole line on which all the pieces are sitting.

Jess: No wonder you like pins – they make the pieces seem rubbish! They can't really do anything when they are pinned.

Jamie: I know! A great idea I like to use is to pile up on the pinned piece. That way, since it can't move, we can usually win the piece. For example, take a look at this complicated position:

First of all, notice where the pin is.

Jess: I can see it! The black bishop on d5 is pinned. The white rook is pinning it against the black queen.

Jamie: What type of pin is it?

Jess: A relative pin!

Jamie: Well done, Jess! Yes, now if I were to put more pressure on that bishop, since it can't move, I'm likely to win it!

Jess: I see! If I move the white knight to f4, then it'll also be attacking the bishop and, since there are more attackers than defenders, we'll win the bishop!

Jamie: See – I love pins!

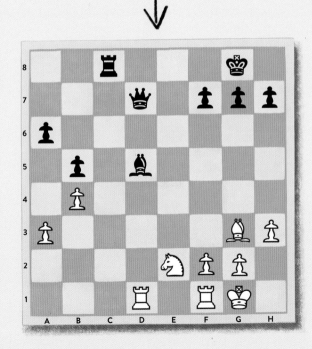

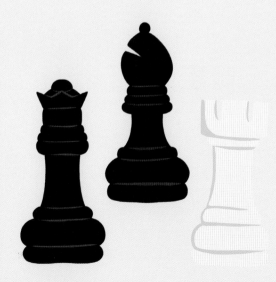

The Skewer

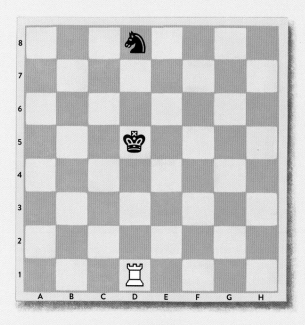

Jess: All this talk about pins has reminded me of a different type of tactic – the skewer.

Jamie: Oh yes, the **reverse pin**! That's the one where it's like a pin, but the more valuable piece is in front, right?

Jess: Yes, it's also known as an **x-ray**. The same line pieces – the queen, rook and bishop – can do a skewer. When they attack a piece, that piece moves out of the way to safety, but there's a piece of lesser or equal value behind it that can also be taken. Look:

This position is just like the one you showed me for the absolute pin, except I've swapped the black pieces around. Now, this is a **skewer**. The king is more valuable as it's worth the entire game. When it moves out of check, to safety, the black knight on d8 can be taken.

Jamie: They are pretty cool, too. I guess it's important to look out for pieces on the same ranks, files and diagonals as your own pieces.

Jess: Yes it is! That's how you spot most tactics! There's another one I want to talk about next, but I'll leave you with a few more skewer examples first.

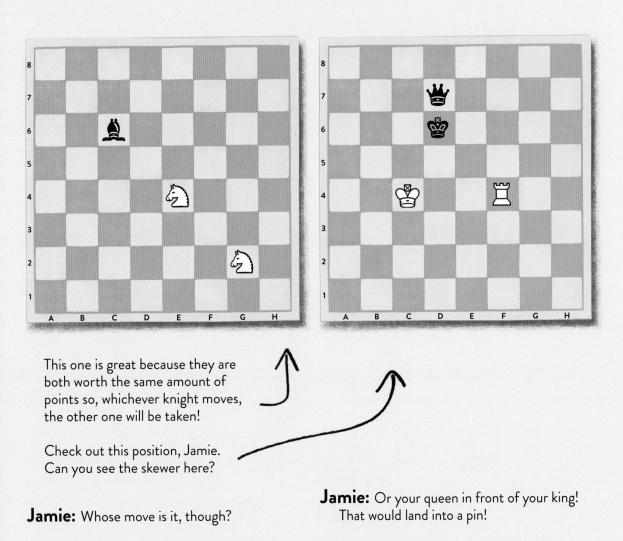

This one is great because they are both worth the same amount of points so, whichever knight moves, the other one will be taken!

Check out this position, Jamie. Can you see the skewer here?

Jamie: Whose move is it, though?

Jess: Doesn't matter – both sides have a skewer. It's a cool example. If it's White's move, he could play his rook to d4. This is an example of why you shouldn't put your king in front of your queen!

Jamie: Or your queen in front of your king! That would land into a pin!

Jess: Good point. The other skewer here would be if it were Black's move. They could play their queen to a4. This would check the white king and, once it has moved, Black could take the rook on f4!

The Discovered Attack or Check

Jamie: The discovered attack or check is definitely one of my favourite tactics. People just don't see it coming and then, BOOM, it hits them!

Jess: I remember! The discovered attack is the one where a piece moves out of the way, but the piece behind it is the one doing the attacking.

Jamie: Yes, I love it! The easy part is spotting the discovered attack, because it's much like the pin or skewer, in which it's a queen, rook or bishop attacking, and there are pieces lined up on the same rank, file or diagonal. The difficult part is deciding where to put the piece that's in the way. Take a look at these examples:

There are three pieces lined up on the d-file. All that's needed to do a discovered attack is for the white knight to be moved. The question is, where should the white knight be moved to?

Jess: The best square is the square that does the most damage, so I'd choose f6 as it attacks the queen!

Jamie: So would I! The queen will definitely be lost! What about this next example?

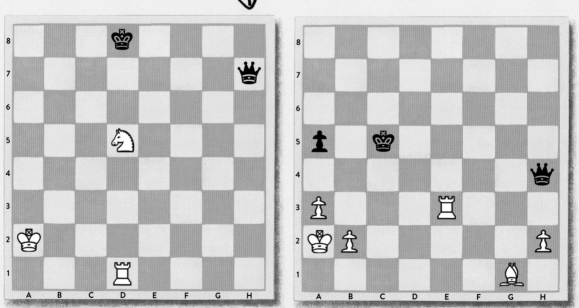

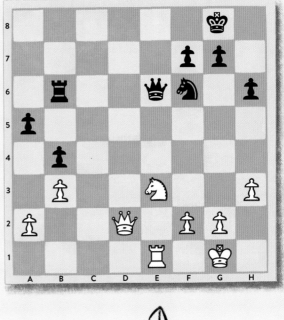

Jess: OK, I know. I can see things lined up on the g1–a7 diagonal. So if I move the rook out of the way, it will be check by the bishop on g1. So I'm gonna move the rook to h3 to attack the queen.

Jamie: Good plan, Jess, but one thing you have to remember is that you should always think about your opponent's plan before you make a move. What do you think Black would do if you played your rook to h3?

Jess: Well, Black could block the check by putting the queen on d4, but I'll take it with my bishop.

Jamie: True, but there's a better move. If you put the rook on e4, then the queen would only be able to block on f2, where you could take it for free.

Jess: Oh, I see, that IS better! I remember a quote from the great **Emanuel Lasker**: 'When you see a good move, look for a better one'. I'll try to do that next time!

Jamie: Both of these examples are of **discovered checks**. I'll now give you one that shows just a **discovered attack**.

Jess: I notice that there's no king exposed to a discovered check, but there are pieces lined up on the e-file. Therefore, I'd like to move the white knight out the way so the black queen will be attacked.

Jamie: OK, but where to?

Jess: Hmm. I think I'll move it to c4 – that's the square that it does the most damage on. Even if they move the queen, I'll take their rook!

Jamie: Yes, that's why discovered attacks are great. Most people will probably not even notice their queen is attacked and just move their rook. Then you get to take their queen!

Removing the Defender

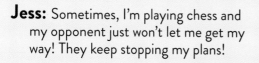

Jess: Sometimes, I'm playing chess and my opponent just won't let me get my way! They keep stopping my plans!

Jamie: Well, what do you expect? They're not just going to let you win, are they?

Jess: That's true, but it's so annoying. There's always a piece stopping me carrying out my plan.

Jamie: Then you should just **remove the defender**.

Jess: I'd love to, but I can't just take it off the board. My opponent would notice! Plus it's not good chess etiquette, remember!

Jamie: Oh, I don't mean like that, silly. I mean it's another tactical device. There are many ways to remove a defender. Like you said, there's often a piece that's stopping you carrying out your plan. If you can get rid of that piece, you can carry out your plan!

Jess: I get you. It sounds like the solution to all my worries. But I'm not sure what to do exactly.

Jamie: OK, I'll give you an example.

You're White; what would you love to do in this position, but can't quite do it right now?

Jess: Take that bishop on e7! So I have to get rid of the queen on d8, right?

Jamie: That's one plan, but there's something a lot more serious that you can do.

Jess: Oh I see – I can almost checkmate on h7 by capturing that pawn with my queen! That annoying knight on f6 is stopping me!

Jamie: Exactly, so just remove it!

Jess: Oh, awesome! I'll just capture it with my bishop! Black can't capture back otherwise it will just be checkmate. Therefore, I'll win material!

Jamie: Spot on! Sometimes, you won't be able to just take the piece, but you may need to chase it away. For example, look at the position below:

In this example, as White, I'd like to capture the rook on f8 with my rook, but the black king is defending it.

Jess: You can't capture the king!

Jamie: I know, so I have to try to get it to move.

Jess: Why don't we check it?

Jamie: That's exactly what we should do.

Jess: But there's an annoying bishop blocking the diagonal on which I want to check the king. Should we remove that defender, too?

Jamie: Good thinking, Jess. Sometimes, we would have to remove a defender to get to another defender, but in this case we can do a **sacrifice**.

Jess: Is that where we give up some material in order to get something better back? Like more material or a checkmate?

Jamie: Exactly. I can use the bishop to capture the pawn on h7, giving check. The black king must move away from the rook. It can take the bishop, but when we take the rook on f8 with the rook on f1 we've gained six points from that combination, whereas Black only gained three.

Jess: Cool! Isn't that kinda like a **deflection**?

Jamie: Yes, sometimes we call it a deflection, but it is a form of removing the defender, too.

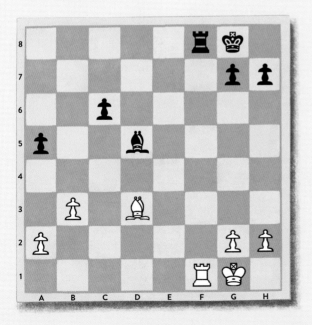

Walking the Dog

Jess: We've learnt so much about the opening and all these cool tactics! But there is no point knowing all of that if we can't finish the game. Therefore, I think it's super important to know all the basic checkmates so we can finish our opponents off!

Jamie: Let's start with an easy one, though. Checkmating with two rooks!

Jess: Oh that should be really easy! You just keep checking and eventually your opponent's king will run out of moves and it will be checkmate. You can even do it with just one rook so I won't need the other!

Jamie: That's not quite right, Jess. You can, indeed, checkmate with one rook, but not by just checking. There are certain techniques that you need to employ. You can't just randomly check the king; you'll need to calculate the moves properly so that you force the king to the edge of the board, where he will soon run out of squares.

Jess: Well, what's that method? I just randomly check and it ends in checkmate.

Jamie: Well, that's fine if your opponents don't know what they're doing, but if they do, that won't work. I'll show you an easy way to do it. First of all, you need to decide which side of the board you want to push the king to, then create an electric fence on the other side so he can't get past. Therefore, in the position on the opposite page, I'd want to push the black king to the 8th rank, so I don't want him to walk forward. Therefore, I want to build my electric fence on the 4th rank. I'll put my rook on c4.

Jess: Oh, that's clever! If the king tries to cross the 4th rank, he will get electrocuted! Therefore he has to go sideways or backward. What if he attacks your rook though, by going to d5?

Jamie: Then you just move as far away from him as possible! Go to h4!

Jess: The electric fence still remains intact!

Jamie: Exactly, so the king still has only half the board to move around in. The next thing I want to do is move the 'spare' rook to the next rank to check the king, pushing him one rank closer to the edge.

Jess: I see the idea. You then keep doing this, rank by rank, and eventually the king will be trapped at the edge of the board.

Jamie: Yes, and this is what we call **Walking the Dog** – as the rooks are 'walking' the king to the edge of the board.

Jess: I've come across this technique before and I thought it was called the 'Lawnmower Checkmate' as it looks as if you are mowing the lawn.

Jamie: It's most commonly known as that, or as the Up the Stairs Mate, but I like to think of it as walking the dog!

Jess: OK, but if the defender knows what they are doing, like you said, then why don't they stop you? For example, in the previous diagram, why can't Black play his king to c5, stopping your other rook checking him?

So what do you do now?

Jamie: Well, there are two ways of handling this. Usually I'd move my rooks as far away as possible from the king, while not disrupting any electric fences, but in this case, our own king is in the way. So I'll move my rook on b1 to b4, so it's defended by the rook on h4. Then, once the king moves, I can check him!

Jess: Ooh, the black king is getting closer to the edge. But, since I know what your plan is, I'll move the black king to c6. Then, if you try to walk the dog and play your rook to h6, I'll just take the rook on b5!

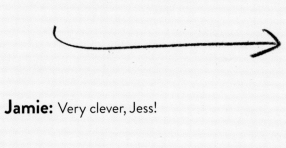

Jamie: Very clever, Jess!

Jess: So what are you going to do about it?

Jamie: Well, I have those two choices I mentioned earlier. I can either move my rook on b5 as far away from the black king as possible, or I can defend it with the other rook.

Jess: OK, so you could either play your rook from h4 to h5 or play your rook on b5 to h5?

Jamie: Actually, I wouldn't move the rook on b5 to h5, even though that's the furthest place away from the king. It gets in the way of the other rook, so I wouldn't be able to walk the dog.

Jess: Oh yeah! How annoying! So you could move it to g5 then, and then on the next go, move the other rook to h6 and check to push the king further back.

Jamie: Exactly, and then keep pushing it until it reaches the end of the board. I'm going to demonstrate what happens if you protect the rook, though.

Now the black king can't capture the rook on b5 as it's protected, so he needs to move away. If he wants to make it as difficult as possible for the rooks, he should stay on the same rank and not voluntarily go backward.

Jess: So perhaps the king should go to d6.

Jamie: Yes, but now we can keep walking the dog. Either rook can go to the 6th rank to check the king and further push him back.

Jess: I'd use my rook on h5 and play it to h6 to check the king. It's much further away, so is safe from the king.

Jamie: Oh, but it doesn't matter because, when the king goes to c7, he will stop our other rook coming down. Look:

Now you can't put your rook on b7, because the king will just take it.

Jess: Can I not just continue the technique you've been using and protect my rook first by moving it from b5 to b6?

Jamie: Yes! That's exactly what you do until you get to the end.

Now here, it's Black to play and he only has one move – to play his king to d8. Then you can choose which rook you move to the back rank in order to checkmate!

Jess: Great! I'm going to practise that until I've perfected both of those techniques. I presume I can do the same thing with a rook and a queen, or even two queens?

Jamie: Huh?! Two queens? You only get one queen at the start of the game!

Jess: But you can promote a pawn to a second queen. You can even have nine queens at a time!

Jamie: No way!

Jess: Yes way, if you promote all eight pawns and keep your original queen.

Jamie: I suppose so. Well, the same techniques apply, but they are just a bit easier with the queen, because the defending king will have fewer squares it can go to.

Jess: Right, I'm off to practise!

The Kiss of Death

Jess: Jamie, if it's easier to walk the dog with the queen than the rook, because the king's squares are more limited, does that mean we can checkmate with just one queen all alone?

Jamie: Yes, it does! Although that's not *quite* correct, because we'll always have our king, since he can't get taken – remember? We can't checkmate with only one queen without the use of our king.

Jess: Do you have a cool technique for this, too?

Jamie: Yes, and it's super easy! I call it the **Shadow Technique**. You don't even need to think while doing it – you just follow the defending king everywhere!

First of all, I move the queen to a square that's a knight's move away from the king, so that she's cutting off lots of squares. In this case, that would be to g4. Look how she cuts off all the squares that the king can go to.

Now you can see the two electric fences, making a box! The general rule for boxing that I have is, if you can make the box smaller, you should. If you can't make the box smaller, move your king. It always works!

Jamie: OK, I'm going to try. If Black moves to e5, then I'll move my rook to d4, making the box smaller.

Jess: That's right. Now just do that all the way until the king gets near the corner. That's when you need to be a little bit careful.

It's Black to play here and they only have one move – to move into the corner. However, if you just follow by my rule and don't calculate, then after you make the box smaller by moving your rook to g7, you'll be in for a shock! It's stalemate!

Jamie: Gosh, I'd better be careful! I'll move my king to g6 instead.

Jess: Good idea. Then, when the king returns to g8 on the next move, we can retreat our rook anywhere along the f-file, ready to meet Black's forced reply Kh8 by rook to f8, which will be checkmate.

Jamie: That one is definitely a lot harder than the other checkmates, but I guess once I practise I'll find it easy.

Jess: Yes, the best way is to practise everything as much as possible. The more you play, the better you get.

Jamie: Are there puzzles that I can solve? I think that would be a fun way to practise!

Jess: Yes, there are loads of places you can get puzzles from – books and online. I think we should include a section of puzzles in this book, too.

Jamie: Good idea!

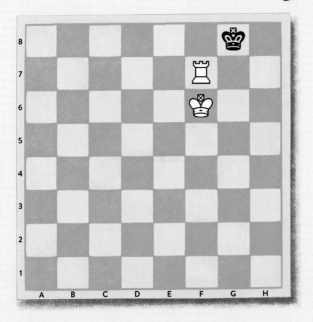

Puzzle Section 1: Winning Material

Jess: I love puzzles. I think they're the best way of practising and keeping our minds in shape.

Jamie: Me too! Let's start with different ways to win material. The aim is to find the correct combination to win material (using notation) and then name the correct type of tactic used. It is White to play in each diagram.

Jess: Sounds easy enough! Let's see those puzzles!

Puzzle 1

Puzzle 2

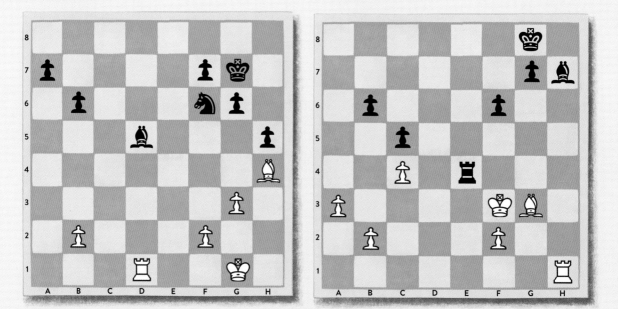

Puzzle 3

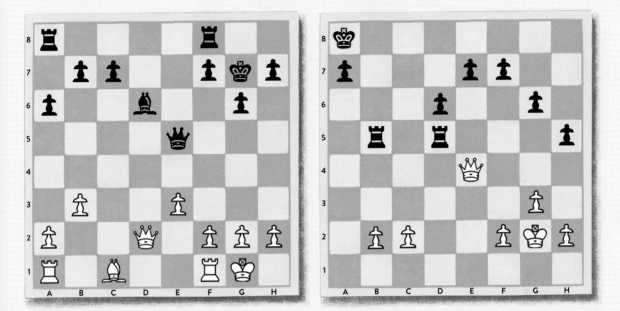

Puzzle 4

Puzzle 5

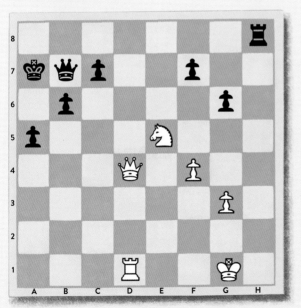

Puzzle 6

Winning Material Answers

Puzzle 1

This is a **Removing the defender** tactic. We would like to take the bishop on d5, but it's currently protected by the knight on f6. So if we take the knight on f6 first, we can take the bishop afterwards.

Puzzle 2

This is also a **removing the defender** trick. However, this time, it's not check and you are not exchanging. This also involves a **sacrifice**. The rook on e4 is vulnerable and the only piece defending it is the bishop on h7. We can make a temporary sacrifice of a rook, as we'll regain the rook on e4 afterwards.

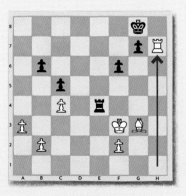

Answer: Bxf6+

Answer: Rxh7

Puzzle 3

White needs to be careful here as Black is threatening ...Qxh2, which is checkmate! The tactic here is a **pin**. Remember we should always be looking out for pieces on the same ranks, files or diagonals. In this diagram, the black king and queen are on the same diagonal and so there's a pin there that will win the queen.

Answer: Bb2

Puzzle 4

This puzzle involves both a **fork** and a **pin**. The white queen is pinning the black rook on d5, so it can't move. It's protected at the moment by the rook on b5. We should be looking to exploit the pin by attacking the pinned piece. We can do this here and it forks the two rooks at the same time.

Answer: c4

Puzzle 5

This is an example of both a **sacrifice** and a **discovered attack**. The black rook on h8 is lonely and undefended. However, it's doing a good job – it's supporting the black queen coming to h1 and checkmating the white king. White has a great tactic here, though, in which the knight can block the path of the knight and reveal an attack on the black rook.

Answer: Nc6+

Puzzle 6

This puzzle also has different tactics. There's a **sacrifice** and a **discovered attack**. There could also be a **royal fork**, depending on which move you choose. The black queen is undefended again, and once the white knight moves, the white queen will be attacking it. Remember, we always look for the most dangerous place. In this case, we should check the black king. This can be done both on g5 or f6. If on f6, it will fork the black king and queen and be a royal fork.

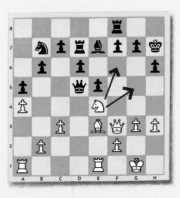

Answer: Ng5+ or Nf6+

Puzzle Section 2: Mate in One

Jamie: How did you find those puzzles, Jess?

Jess: Very easy! But I'd like to practise checkmating, not just winning pieces.

Jamie: OK, that makes sense, since that's how you win a game of chess! Here are some 'Mate in One' puzzles.

Jess: Is that where I have to checkmate immediately with just one move?

Jamie: Yes! It's White to play in all of them again. I'll give you one clue – the first puzzle is a bit of trick question.

Puzzle 1

Puzzle 2

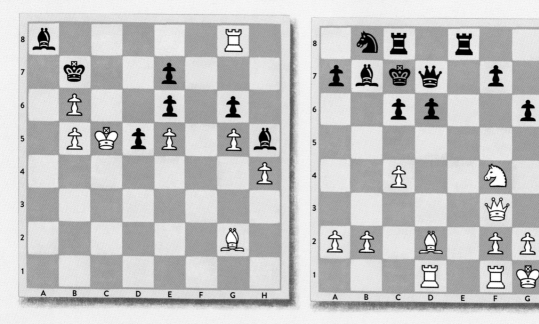

Puzzle 3

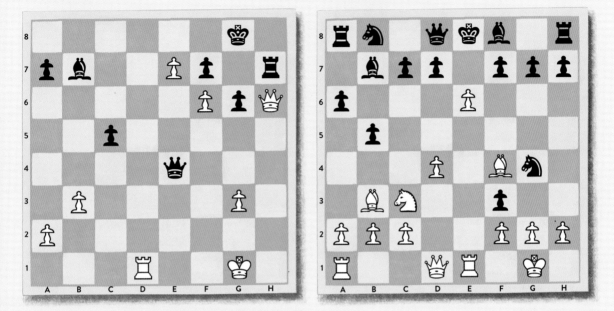

Puzzle 4

Puzzle 5

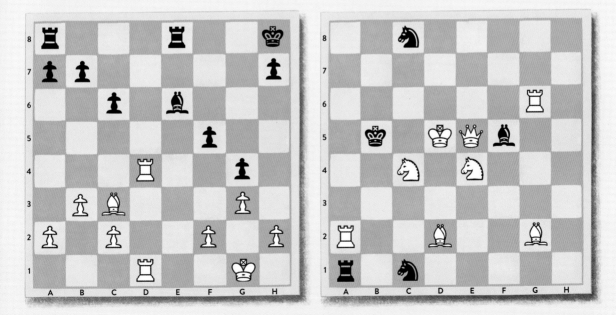

Puzzle 6

Mate in One Answers

Puzzle 1

Remember this one was a trick puzzle. As we can see, there are only two checks in this position, Rb8+ and Bxd5+. However, both of these moves lead to the pieces being taken, therefore we have to wonder how on earth it's possible to checkmate in just one move. Two moves, sure, but not one move! Think back to all those special moves we learnt. After all, it has to be special to produce a mate in one here. Yes, **en passant**!

Answer: exd5 e.p #

Puzzle 2

This one is an easier one – just keeping looking for checks. Once you've found one that doesn't lose a piece, check that the black king can't go anywhere.

Answer: Ba5#

Puzzle 3

A good tip while looking for checkmates when your queen is on the board is 'look for the closest place next to the king, where it is safe'. Often, this can lead to checkmate or the best check. It applies to this puzzle. The white queen can't go to g7, despite the king being unable to capture it, because the black rook can capture it. Therefore...

Answer: Qf8#

Puzzle 4

This is a clever **discovered check** and a **double check**. Remember always to look for pieces on the same files. The black king is uncastled and on the same file as White's rook. That's never a good sign. White can deliver a double check to checkmate.

Answer: exf7#

Puzzle 5

Again there's another **discovered check**, but this time it's not a double check. The white rook needs to be moved out of the way for the black king to be in danger, but the key square is where? There's no double check, so the rook should go to the square where it covers the most escape squares. Remember that it doesn't matter if the piece is in danger, because it is check.

Answer: Rxg4#

Puzzle 6

This is a bit of a crazy position and there's so much going on everywhere. When the situation is like this, you have to think about which pieces are doing what. You don't want to move a piece that is covering lots of escape squares. If you look, the white queen is doing the least. The black king can't move anywhere at the moment, so that means the next check will be checkmate, as long as you don't move a crucial piece. When you realise the queen needs to give check, you must make sure that check can't be blocked. Then, you'll notice the clever move.

You may think that the king can't checkmate, but if it's a **discovered check**, the last move can be checkmate, even if it is a king move!

Answer: Kd4#

Jess: That was really clever and I learnt a lot! I'd love to see how the masters of the game played, because I think I could really learn a lot from them!

Jamie: Well, I'll show you a game by one the earlier great chess players. He was an American Master called Paul Morphy.

Jess: Great! I can't wait!

Master Game

Paul Morphy
vs
Count Isouard and the Duke of Brunswick

Paul Morphy was one of the greatest players of all time and was known for his attacking genius. This game was played in very weird conditions. In October 1859, two aristocrats, the Duke of Brunswick and Count Isouard, were at a performance of the opera *The Barber of Seville* when they decided to have a game of chess. They were both amateurs but didn't play too badly. It just so happened that Paul Morphy was at that same opera, and they challenged him to a game during the interval!

White: Paul Morphy

Black: Count Isouard and the Duke of Brunswick

1. e4 e5 2. Nf3 d6 3. d4 Bg4
Already, Black has gone slightly wrong.
This move is inaccurate as it leads to
the immediate loss of the two bishops.
The so-called 'Bishop Pair' has all the
strengths of one bishop, but none of
its weaknesses, as together the two
bishops control all the squares on the
chessboard. Thus here it is better to
retain both bishops by playing the more
accurate 3...Nf6 or 3...Nd7.

4. dxe5 Bxf3 Now the bishop must
be given up as after 4...dxe5 5. Qxd8+
Kxd8 6. Nxe5 and White
has won a pawn.

5. Qxf3 dxe5
Only five moves
have been played,
and White already
has an advantage in
development and the
bishop pair.

6. Bc4 As well as threatening the obvious
Qxf7#, this move develops a bishop to
a strong diagonal and threatens Qb3 to
double on the diagonal.

6...Nf6 7. Qb3! This move forks the pawns
on b7 and on f7. Already Black is in trouble.

7...Qe7 This might look like a strange move,
but the idea behind it is that Black is being
attacked by some strong White pieces, so
Black is looking to swap off the pieces so
that he will be in less danger.

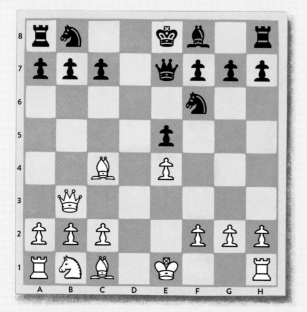

Black is hoping that after 8. Qxb7, he can play 8...Qb4+ and swap off the queens and hinder White's attack.

White has several choices here to take an advantage, but Morphy stuck to the general opening principles and decided not to pawn-grab, but continued with the development of his pieces by **8. Nc3!** Black saw this as an opportunity to defend his pawn and played **8...c6**

9. Bg5 and now all of White's minor pieces are developed. **9...b5?** Black has totally neglected his development – he WILL be punished for this.

So what should the Duke have done instead? Perhaps 9...Qc7 would have been a better try, because this queen is blocking in the dark-squared bishop and hindering Black's development. This move would allow Black's pieces to be a little more co-ordinated. Of course, White still has the advantage, but it wouldn't be so decisive as in the game.

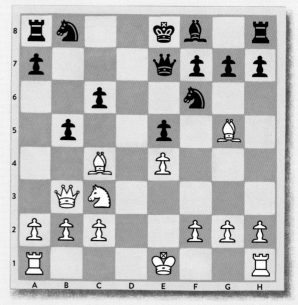

10. Nxb5!! Paul Morphy sees how weak the Duke's light squares are now his light-squared bishop is gone, and uses this opportunity to control them with his own light-squared bishop!

10...cxb5 11. Bxb5+ Nbd7 12. 0-0-0!

What a way to get another piece into the attack! Morphy is now threatening to capture on d7, since the black knight on f6 is pinned.

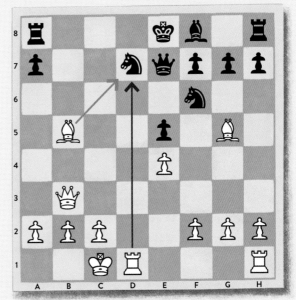

12...Rad8 Desperately trying to defend! Other tries such as 12...Qb4 don't work, despite getting out of the pin to allow the f6 knight to defend. The tactic of 'Removing the Defender' allows 13. Bxf6 and then winning a piece as the d7 square will no longer be defended. Even 13...Qxb3 loses to 14. Bxd7#!!

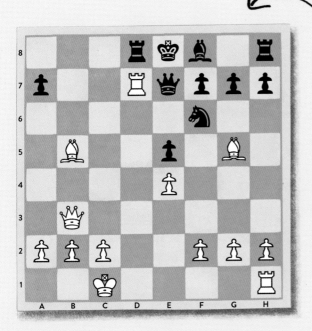

13. Rxd7! A typical Morphy move – sacrificing to destroy his opponent's defences.

So Morphy's sacrifice this time is temporary, as after 13...Rxd7, the black rook is still pinned, so can be taken anytime. But did Morphy really have to be so flashy about it? What if he decided to just slowly build up on the d-file with 13. Rd2 and 14. Rhd1? The problem is that Black can then play a move like 13...Qb4 to swap off the queens and reduce the number of attacking pieces, or perhaps 13...h6 and try to annoy the pinning bishop.

Morphy's move may indeed look a bit over-the-top, but it's an extremely effective and sound sacrifice.

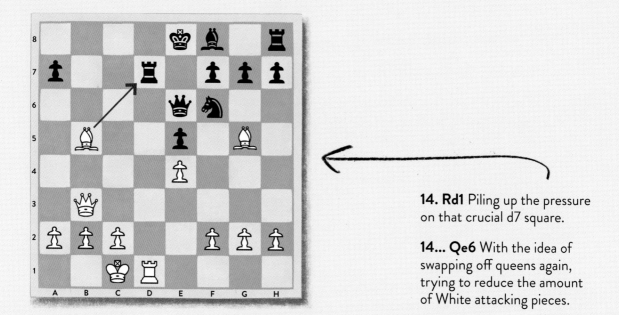

14. Rd1 Piling up the pressure on that crucial d7 square.

14... Qe6 With the idea of swapping off queens again, trying to reduce the amount of White attacking pieces.

However, Black has missed a spectacular finish: **15. Bxd7+** forking the black king and queen. Seeing this, Black didn't want to lose his queen and so recaptured with **15... Nxd7.**

The Count and Duke certainly didn't expect the final blow of: **16. Qb8+!!**

A magnificent sacrifice, forcing **16...Nxb8** and so finishing with **17. Rd8.** Checkmate!

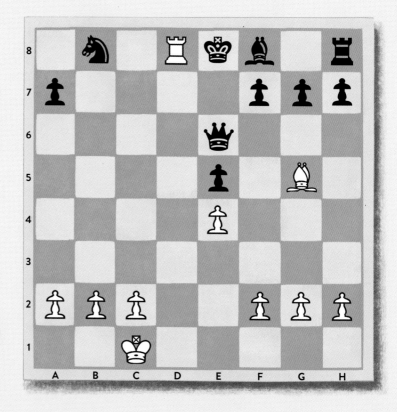

Jess: Wow, Jamie, that was amazing! However, it was rather complicated! I think I need to brush up on my notation first.

Jamie: Yes, I agree. This is how professionals analyse.

Jess: Wow, thanks Jamie. I'm going to use the notation sheets at the back of the book every time I play a game, even with you, Jamie!

Jamie: Good idea!

Jess: Well I hope that everyone has enjoyed this book and have learnt lots. I know I have!

Jamie: And I know I have!

Jess: If you are stuck on anything, please just read over the chapter again and again, and soon you'll be winners!

Goodbye everyone!

Notation Sheet

Event: **Date:**   **Result:**

White:

Black:

#	White	Black	#	White	Black
1			26		
2			27		
3			28		
4			29		
5			30		
6			31		
7			32		
8			33		
9			34		
10			35		
11			36		
12			37		
13			38		
14			39		
15			40		
16			41		
17			42		
18			43		
19			44		
20			45		
21			46		
22			47		
23			48		
24			49		
25			50		

Glossary

3-fold repetition A type of draw. It occurs when the exact same position has occurred three times in the game. It does not have to be the same three moves in a row, but the same position.

50-move rule A type of draw. It occurs when 50 moves for each side have been played, with no captures or pawn moves.

ABC of Check The three different ways to get out of check. A = Avoid, B = Block, C = Capture.

Absolute pin A type of pin in which the pinned piece can't move, because to move would be illegal.

Achilles' Heel The heel of a Greek hero. It is used to describe the f7 square in Black's starting line-up or the f2 square in White's starting line-up. It is a very weak spot in the army at the start of the game.

Advantageous exchange An exchange of pieces from which one side gains material. It is advantageous to the side who got the better pieces.

Attack When one piece is in the line of fire of another piece. The piece can be attacked but not necessarily threatened (see **threat**).

Battery More than one piece controlling the same rank, file or diagonal.

Bishop pair When a player has two bishops and their opponent does not, there is a slight advantage for the bishop pair. Together they have all the strengths of a bishop, but none of the weaknesses.

Box mate The technique used when you are trying to checkmate a lone king with just a rook and a king. The idea is to cut the defending king's squares off, gradually, until he is trapped on the edge of the board.

Bull's head An ideal opening structure. Following the three golden rules of the opening, this is the sort of position we would aim for because it controls the centre of the board and all our pieces are placed nicely for attack, while our king is safely castled.

Castling The special move done with the king and rook in order to get the king safe. The rook and king do not swap, but the king moves two squares and the rook jumps over.

Check When the king is attacked. He must get out of check immediately.

Checkmate When the king is trapped and the ABC of Check does not work. The king must be in check, or it is stalemate.

Complement When two pieces work together well, they are said to complement each other.

Deflection A type of the tactic in which an attack is made on a defender (see **Removing the defender**). Deflection is when you drive the defender away to another square where it can't do its defensive job anymore.

Diagonal The angled straight line from one corner to another of the chessboard. It is along these that the bishops must travel.

Discovered attack/check A discovered attack is when a player moves a piece out of the way to reveal an attack from another of his pieces that was behind it. A discovered check is the same principle, but the revealed piece is producing a check.

Double attack When two pieces are being attacked at the same time. This is also known as a **fork**.

Double check A double check can only occur from a **discovered check**. It is when a king is in check by two different pieces.

Ending The third stage of the game. Not many pieces are left on the board and the game will shortly come to an end.

En passant A special move in which, when a white (black) pawn reaches the fifth (fourth) rank, it gets to capture pawns in a different way – it can now capture a pawn that goes past it as if it has only moved one square.

Etiquette Good behaviour. You should behave in a certain way when playing chess.

Exchange 1. To swap pieces of equal value. 2. The advantage of a rook for a knight or a bishop.

Family fork An attack on a king, queen and rook at the same time.

File The vertical rows of squares on the chessboard, named after letters.

Fork When one piece attacks more than one piece at the same time.

Insufficient material A type of draw. One side is left with not enough material to win the game. The other side will have just a king. The game will then be drawn.

Kingside The four **files** on the right-hand side of the board – the side the king is on.

Kiss of death The checkmate produced after the shadow technique is used, just using a queen and king.

Lawnmower The checkmating technique using two rooks and a king versus a king. We call it 'Walking the Dog' in this book.

Line pieces The pieces that control whole lines – the queen, the rooks and the bishops.

Material Refers to pieces or points.

Middlegame The second stage of the game. This is when most of the action occurs. It is the stage just after all of the pieces have been developed and when the two sides make plans.

Minor pieces The knights and the bishops.

Notation The moves of the game, written down to record them.

Opening The first stage of the game, in which the initial aim is to get the pieces out as quickly as possible and to castle.

Opposition The situation in which both kings are opposite each other, one square apart. Whoever gains the opposition has the advantage. It is something used in endings.

Pin Where a piece is pinned to a square and cannot move. There are two type of pin – see **absolute pin** and **relative pin**.

Promotion When a pawn gets to the end of the board and can choose which piece it wants to turn into.

Queenside The four files on the left-hand side of the board – the side where the queen is situated.

Rank The horizontal lines going across the board, named after numbers.

Relative Pin A type of pin in which a piece is in front of a more valuable piece and if it's moved, the piece behind it would be taken. The piece in front isn't absolutely pinned, because it can move, but if it did, it would be a bad idea.

Removing the defender A very common tactic in games. There are several ways of trying to remove the defender, but if you have a plan and something is defending it, get rid of that piece! You can capture the piece, deflect it, lure it away, etc.

Sacrifice When you give up some material for a much better gain. For example, if you give away your queen to ensure that you can checkmate your opponent.

Scholar's Mate Also known as the 4-move checkmate.

Skewer Like a reverse pin, but where a more valuable piece is in front of a less valuable piece. When the more valuable piece moves to safety, the one behind can be captured.

Stalemate Another type of draw, in which the player in turn has no legal moves left and is not in check.

Strategy The technique used in chess to help plan and make decisions.

Tactics The tricks and traps used in chess to try to win material.

Threat When there is an attack that can be executed on the next go. A threat is something that should be dealt with immediately.

Touch Move/Take A tournament rule – if you touch a piece, you must move it. Likewise, if you touch one of your opponent's pieces, you must take it if you can.

Under-promotion When a pawn gets to the end of the board and promotes to any other piece than a queen.

X-ray Also known as a **skewer**.

Index

Sabrina Chevannes is a Women's International Chess Master
and digital marketing professional. She started playing chess
at 8 years old and has won 10 British chess titles.